Global Perspectives Series

Voices from the Margins

Langham
GLOBAL LIBRARY

Voices from the Margins

Wisdom of Primal Peoples in the Era of World Christianity

Edited by

Jangkholam Haokip and David W. Smith

Published 2022 by Langham Global Library
An imprint of Langham Publishing
www.langhampublishing.org

Langham Publishing and its imprints are a ministry of Langham Partnership

Langham Partnership
PO Box 296, Carlisle, Cumbria, CA3 9WZ, UK
www.langham.org

ISBNs:
978-1-83973-534-9 Print
978-1-83973-695-7 ePub
978-1-83973-696-4 Mobi
978-1-83973-697-1 PDF

British Library Cataloguing-in-Publication Data
A catalogue record for this book is available from the British Library

ISBN: 978-1-83973-534-9

Cover & Book Design: projectluz.com

Contents

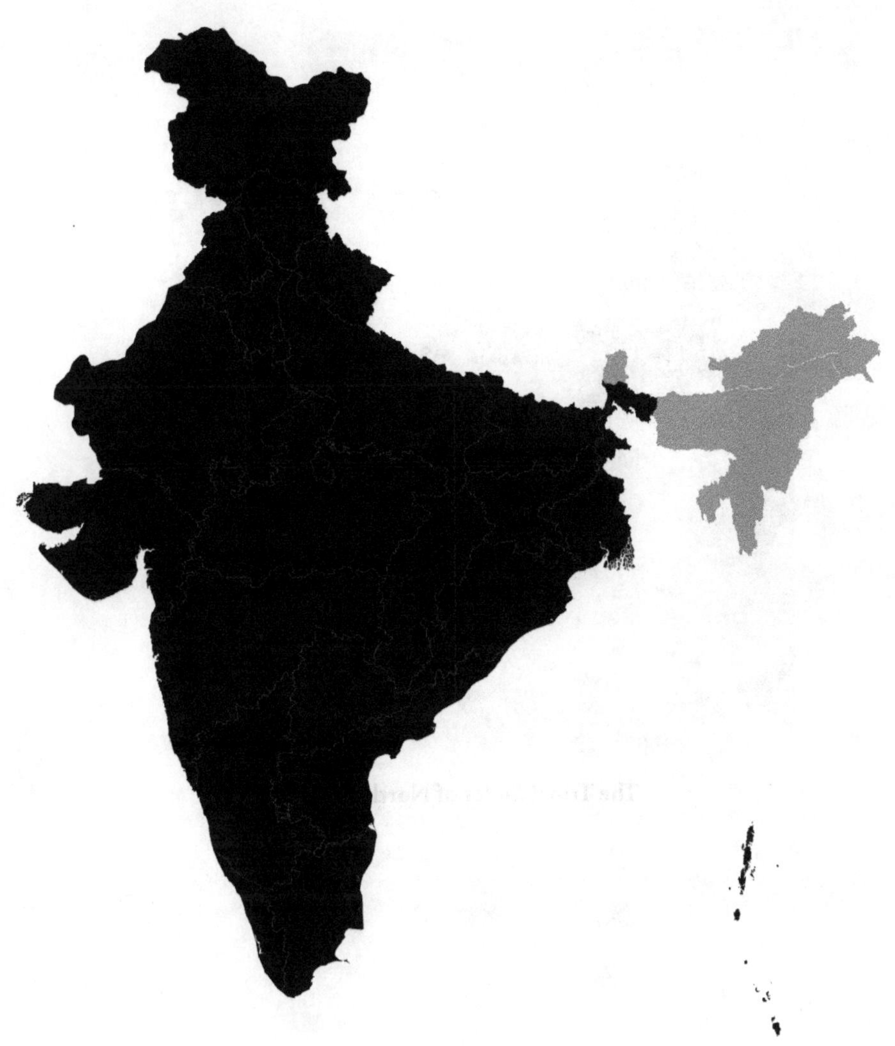

The Indian Subcontinent, Highlighting the Northeast Region[1]

1. Taken from: https://commons.wikimedia.org/wiki/File:North_East_India.svg, Nilabh12, CC by-SA 4.0.

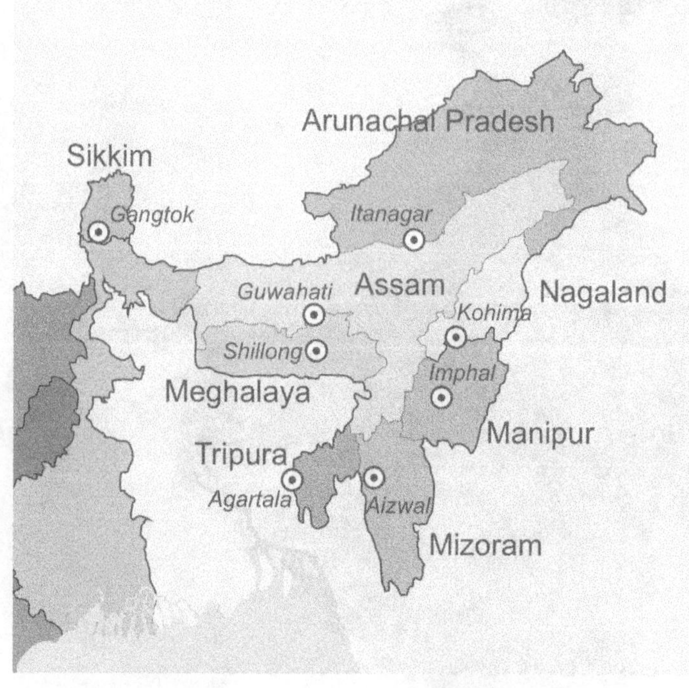

The Tribal States of Northeast India[2]

2. Taken from: from: https://en.wikipedia.org/wiki/Northeast_India, Renzut, CC by-SA 4.0.

Introduction

The studies contained in this book emerged from a series of discussions which took place in Northeast India during 2019 in connection with the birth of the Bethesda Khankho Institute in the state of Manipur. Some explanation is needed of the book's title which identifies the voices recorded here as being "from the margins." A glance at the map of modern India will be enough to indicate that geographically this region is indeed "marginal" in a physical sense in that it is distant from the bulk of the Indian subcontinent and connected to it by a very thin strip of land. As an Indian commentator observes, since 1947 the Northeast has been "all but physically separated" from the rest of India, becoming "virtually landlocked, like Nepal and Bhutan, with under one percent of its external boundaries contiguous with the rest of India."[1]

However, the physical isolation of the peoples of Northeast India is only one factor in their marginalisation, since historically, culturally, and religiously they have been shaped by experiences which set them apart from the majority population of the nation state to which they belong. The story is far too complex to be described here, but as will become evident in what follows, the term most often used within India to describe the peoples of the Northeast is "tribal." They share this identity with many other groups elsewhere on the subcontinent, but only here do they constitute the majority of the population and possess some degree of political power.

Added to these causes of the marginalisation of the peoples of the Northeast is the nature of their religious history and identity. The traditional religions of the original inhabitants of this part of the world have been described in various ways at different times from being classified as "animist" and "pagan" during the colonial period, when their traditional beliefs were frequently treated with disdain and seen as a mark of backwardness, to the more neutral language often used today in terminology such as "traditional" or "primal" religions. The coming of Christianity through the agency of Western missionaries frequently resulted in the displacement of centuries-old traditional beliefs and practices which were invariably regarded as inconsistent with the new loyalty to Christ, and therefore were required to be abandoned as part of the cost of conversion.

1. B. G. Verghese, *India's Northeast Resurgent: Ethnicity, Insurgency, Governance, Development* (Delhi: Konark, 1997), xii.

The book you hold in your hands is but one piece of evidence of a remarkable shift now occurring on a global scale in the perception of traditional religions. This shift includes new perspectives on African traditional religions, as is made clear by the presence of James R. Krabill's contribution, and recognition of the important role of "marginal" people to an emergent "world Christianity," which also becomes clear in the following pages. There are significant challenges here for Christians in the Western world, especially with regard to understanding the distinctive nature of oral traditions. But the central theme of the book concerns the recovery and transmission of the indigenous knowledge of the peoples of Northeast India. Many of our authors wrestle with the crucial challenge of contextualising the gospel in relation to their own languages, cultures, and traditions. They also demonstrate, as for example does Fabian Lyngdoh in his discussion of contextualisation among the Khasi people in chapter seven, that tribal peoples do not perceive themselves to be marginal to a wider society, whether that be India or the culture of modernity stemming from the Western world, but rather they identify their location to be "in the centre of the earth, in their own homeland . . . with the navel of heaven right in their midst."

It becomes clear that the studies contained in this volume reflect on the growing realisation that recurring economic and social crises across the world threaten the very survival of the earth in all its beauty and variety, and that the wisdom embedded in "indigenous knowledge" has something vital to offer people far beyond the Northeast of India. These millennia-old traditions contain wisdom which can enrich an emergent world Christianity, but which may also contribute important insights to broader debates concerning the pressing ecological, social, and political issues arising in the era of globalization. In an important academic study of religious thought and political practice in Africa, Stephen Ellis and Gerrie ter Haar observe that Europeans tend to argue that "spiritual knowledge is best confined to private space or is applicable to specific cultures only." Yet at the same time, those who propound such views affirm belief in democracy and free markets, "neither of them any more visible than spirits," and claim for them "universal application." However, there are clear indications that such bias is increasingly being challenged even within Western academia as the looming crises confronting the world have sparked "a massively important debate about what types of knowledge are appropriate and applicable to whom."[2]

2. Stephen Ellis and Gerrie ter Haar, *Worlds of Power: Religious Thought and Political Practice in Africa* (London: Hurst, 2004), 195.

What all of this means is that peoples who are often overlooked because of their "marginal" status are now finding their voices and believe that they have something important to say to the human family as a whole. As an important statement from the World Council of Churches has reminded us, we are today facing a radically changing Christian landscape "described as 'world Christianity' where the majority of Christians are either living, or having their origins in the global South or East." At the same time, "people at the margins are claiming their key role as the agents of mission and affirming mission as transformation."[3] As one of us has noted elsewhere, there is a growing global quest for values that respect difference "and affirm the human dignity of all peoples." This present book constitutes part of that quest as it is occurring at the present time in Northeast India, and it contributes "to the voices of primal peoples around the globe" who offer their values "to the well-being of the human family as a whole." What was once silenced as primitive needs to be given a chance to speak for the good of all.[4]

Jangkholam Haokip
David W. Smith

---

3. World Council of Churches, "Together Towards Life," in *Ecumenical Visions for the Twenty First Century*, eds. Melisande Lorke and Dietrich Werner (Geneva: WCC Publications, 2013), 192.

4. Jangkholam Haokip, *Can God Save My Village? A Theological Study of Identity among the Tribal People of Northeast India with Special Reference to the Kukis of Manipur* (Carlisle: Langham, 2014), 312.

Contributors

Rocelyn Anog-Madinger is SIL Philippines Ethno-Arts Consultant and President of the Institute for Orality Strategies.

Songram Basumatary is Principal of the Gurukul Lutheran Theological College and Research Institute, Chennai.

Peter Haokip is a Catholic priest of the Archdiocese of Imphal, Manipur. He has taught Bible, Latin, Hebrew, and tribal theology at Oriens Theological College, Shillong.

Jangkholam Haokip is Founder and Director of Bethesda Khankho Institute in Manipur, pursuing research in indigenous knowledge and traditions in the context of world Christianity.

James R. Krabill is Core Adjunct Professor at Anabaptist Mennonite Biblical Seminary, Elkhart, Indiana, USA.

Fabian Lyngdoh is former Professor and Head of the Centre for Cultural Study and Community Initiatives at Martin Luther Christian University, Shillong.

Charles Madinger is Founder and CEO of the Institute for Orality Strategies (IOS) and Director of the International Orality Network.

David W. Smith is Honorary Lecturer in the School of Divinity, History and Philosophy at the University of Aberdeen, Scotland, UK.

Donovan Swer is Assistant Professor of Music at Martin Luther Christian University, Shillong.

Maribon Vinay is Research Dean and Associate Professor of Psychology at Martin Luther Christian University, Shillong.

Virginius Xaxa is Visiting Professor at the Institute for Human Development, New Delhi.

Elungkiebe Zeliang is Associate Professor and Head of the Department of Conflict Management and Peace Initiatives at Martin Luther Christian University, Shillong.

Part One

Primal Traditions and Christianity

Historical and Missiological Perspectives

1

The Tribal Peoples of Northeast India

Virginius Xaxa

India is a vast country. In fact, many have described it as the subcontinent. Given its vastness, India has often been discussed and studied in reference to its regions such as Northern, Southern, Western, Eastern, and Northeastern. What is referred to as the Northeast, or the Northeastern region, was originally comprised of the seven states of Assam, Arunachal Pradesh, Meghalaya, Manipur, Mizoram, Nagaland, and Tripura. This section constituted eight percent of India's geographical area and a little less than four percent of the total population of the country.[1] Sikkim was added to the region in 2002. The entry of Sikkim with its 7,096 square kilometres of territory makes up three percent of the total geographical area of the region.[2] Unlike the Southern, Northern, Western, etc. regions, which remain more geographical notions, and despite some distinct linguistic and cultural configurations, the Northeast has moved beyond being merely geographical territory. Today it has been transformed to a distinct politico-administrative category. This process began with the setting up of the Northeast Council (NEC) in 1972 which was established as a statutory advisory body under the NEC Act the previous year. The aims were to secure balanced and coordinated development and to facilitate coordination among the states. Since 2002, however, the NEC has been mandated as the Regional

1. Venkata Rao, *A Century of Government and Politics in North East India,* vol. 1 (New Delhi: S. Chand, 1983), 1.

2. North Eastern Council Secretariat, Basic Statistics of North Eastern region 2015 (Shillong: Directorate of Printing & Stationery, Government of Meghalaya, 2015), xxviii.

Planning Body for the region. The idea of a region was further solidified with the setting up of the Northeast Development Financial Institution (NEDFI) in 1995 and a separate ministry for development of the region in 2001 known as the Ministry of Development of Northeast Region (MDoNER). The former aimed at all-round development of the region while the latter acted as the nodal agency between central government and the states in the region. With the establishment of these agencies, there has been a separate allocation of budget for the Northeast.

The emergence of the Northeast as a distinct region in the forms mentioned above can be traced to the politics of the region since the 1960s. This being the case, there has been quite a shift in the way the Northeast is viewed from so-called mainland India today. The region was earlier seen primarily as one inhabited by a diversity of tribal groups with distinct languages, cultures, and traditions; in fact in the shaping of the idea of the Northeast as a region, tribes and tribal politics seemed to have played a pivotal role. It was the movements of tribal identity and autonomy engulfing the region in the 1960s and early 1970s which led the Indian state to think of the region in a very different way. This is the political context within which the Northeast in its present form is to be understood.

The emergence of the Northeast as a distinct region is a political construct of the Indian state, and hence it is a creation from above. Notwithstanding this construct, the Northeast has become an important category of reference. But such identity has yet to become crystallized in the economic, social, cultural, and political spheres. It is only outside of Northeast India, which is to say in mainland India, that such an identity comes to the surface and, when the situation arises, involves striking racial prejudice and violence against the peoples of Northeast India. By being categorised as a distinct region, the Northeast has caught the attention of the people at large and has become an important reference point for debate and discussion, which is evident in news reporting, academic writing, and the organization of seminars and conferences by universities, NGOs, and other similar organizations. Thus it is the region and regional context that seems to dominate the thinking about the Northeast, and this thinking tends to homogenize the enormous geographic, linguistic, and cultural diversity that marks the region. In short, using the category "tribes" as a lens in looking at the Northeast has been side-lined or subsumed under the broader category of "region." The depth of this regional identity in the social, cultural, and political consciousness of the people is altogether another story.

Political and Administrative Location of Tribes

The Northeast shares over twelve percent of the total tribal population of India. Tribal peoples as percentages of the overall populations of individual states in the Northeast according to the 2011 census are indicated in the following table.[3]

Northeast State	Tribal Percentage
Mizoram	94
Nagaland	87
Meghalaya	86
Arunchal Pradesh	69
Manipur	35
Tripura	32
Sikkim	34
Assam	12

Whereas tribes form substantial majorities in the first four states, in the other four they form a minority. The first four are often described as tribal states because the tribes themselves govern the states, while in the remaining four, non-tribal people govern, and the voices of the tribes remain at the margins. To address this anomaly, the tribes in these states have been provided with some space to govern themselves in the form of autonomous districts and regional councils under the sixth schedule provision of the Indian constitution, with the exception of Manipur. Sikkim, by contrast, has no provision for autonomous councils of any type. These autonomous councils are like mini-states with legislative, executive, and judicial power. However, such power is absent in councils that have been provided under state laws. The autonomous councils in Manipur fall into this category despite strong demands by the tribal groups of the state for the councils to be under the sixth schedule.

The two kinds of political arrangements described above give rise to different sets of problems in the regional tribal situation. In Nagaland, which refused inclusion within the framework of sixth schedule provisions, the special constitutional provision in the form of Article 371-A specifies that no act of parliament should apply to the state in respect to religious or social practices, customary law procedures, administration of civil and criminal law, and ownership of land and resources. Article 371-G provides similar safeguards to Mizoram, although it comes under the sixth schedule. Arunachal Pradesh,

3. Government of India, Ministry of Tribal Affairs, "Statistical Profile of Scheduled Tribes in India" (2013), https://tribal.nic.in/ST/StatisticalProfileofSTs2013.pdf. Accessed 4 October 2019.

Assam, and Manipur have also been provided with additional constitutional provision in the form of Articles 371-H, 371-B, and 371-C respectively.[4]

Emergence of Tribal Identity and Articulation

Since the onset of colonial rule, tribal societies have undergone a transformation, and in the Northeast in the postcolonial period, this change has been faster and wider than elsewhere in India. The three key players in this transformation have been the state, the market, and religion, the latter in the form of Christianity. The state brought different tribes under a single administrative structure and broadly under the same set of laws and rules. Through the construction of roads, railways, and other means of communication and transport, the state also brought together different villages, tribes, and peoples who had been segregated by geographical distance. This connection contributed to the creation of new social bonds, while at the same time the extension of roads and communication facilities opened up the region to the outside world. The infrastructure also stimulated trade and commerce which has gradually changed the tribal economy's system of production, distribution, and consumption. Further, the introduction of the new religion of Christianity not only drew the tribal peoples to new forms of worship, rites, and rituals, but also created new values and norms and added a new sense of identity, since Christian missions introduced modern education and in the process gave script to tribal languages. Those who availed themselves of modern education had the opportunity to move to non-agricultural and non-manual occupations as teachers, catechists, or pastors, and later found work as lower-level government employees in state administrations. These modern institutions have grown manifold in modern India, and with the spread of education, more and more people began to move to new occupations.

Developments such as these opened up the space for social interactions beyond kinship and village structures and paved the way for larger social solidarity and identity. The emergence of new social bonds in the form of distinct tribe/ethnic groups, or generic tribal groups such as the Naga, Zo etc., have resulted from processes which had their genesis under colonial rule. The next step was articulating quests for a distinct identity which resulted in self-determination movements for either a sovereign state or a state within the Indian union. Indeed, the distinct political spaces in the forms of state or

4. Tiplut Nongbri, "Country Technical Note on Indigenous Peoples in India with Special Focus on North Eastern Region," A Study Commissioned by and Submitted to Asia Indigenous Peoples Pact, Changmai, Thailand, 2011.

autonomous councils that tribes have been able to create for themselves are the result of a long chain of struggles, some of which have involved violence. Processes such as these have sharpened issues of identity in the region which are manifested in different forms.

Again what marks the tribal population in the Northeast, as elsewhere in India, is their heterogeneity in terms of language/dialect, geography/territory, population size, and religion/denomination. Even more important is that tribal peoples are differently placed in their access to political power and hence have different access to the fruits of development, both economic and social. These issues of uneven development are generally addressed by political empowerment, either in the form of states or some other type of autonomous institution. But uneven development has been an issue even in the case of tribes who enjoy autonomy. Generally, tribes who are numerically and economically dominant and privileged have taken advantage of opportunities, whereas such opportunities have not accrued to numerically smaller groups. In other words, whatever developmental process has been at work has tended to be exclusionary rather than inclusionary, which leads to articulating distinct identities and tends to create moves in the direction of autonomy. The identity issue in the region has thus become caught in the circle of a web, and there seems to be no way in sight to get out of it.

This identity issue, coupled with disparity in development and political power, has been at the root of various forms of conflict that continue to plague the region. Some of the key forms are conflicts between individuals and communities on their views of customary laws that at times are in contravention of the rights to citizens provided in the constitution. Gender conflict is one example, while interethnic community conflict, which is fairly widespread, has at times turned violent and taken a heavy toll on lives and property. The memory of such conflict still haunts people, and no effort has been made to initiate the process of healing. Additionally, there are the conflicts between natives/locals and outsiders/migrants. There has also been conflict within particular ethnic communities, and cleavage and conflict has occurred between people with different religious affiliations, such as Christians and non-Christians. Even within the same religious community there has been cleavage and tension, such as between Christians along denominational lines. At times these various conflicts have gone to the extent of denying the basic human rights to freedom and even existence. Despite the fact that conflicts are endemic, no serious effort has been made to address these problems in the form of opening up a space for discussion, negotiation, consensus, and peace building.

Economic Differentiation, Inequality, and Urbanization

Alongside the above is the unprecedented economic differentiation among tribes. The region is marked by the prevalence of shifting agriculture which corresponds with clan/lineage and community-based ownership. Of course side by side has been the presence of individual or private ownership of land. However, while clan/lineage and village community still dominate the pattern of ownership, this pattern is steadily changing. The shifting agriculture is giving place to settled forms of agriculture such as terrace rice cultivation, plantation crops such as tea and rubber, and horticulture. With this shift has been an increase in private property formations. The mechanism through which these changes are taking place is not clear; however, with the increase of private property formation, the access of the people at large to community resources is shrinking. This unequal access to resources is paving the way for social inequality in societies that were relatively egalitarian. Inequality in tribal society has been reinforced by the white-collar employment which became possible through access to modern education in general and higher education in particular. Indeed, modern education and political power have been two of the axial principles of social mobility and inequality in tribal society as agriculture declines as an important source of employment. In fact, one finds an unprecedented rise in the number of people drawing their livelihood from sources other than agriculture. The service sector has become dominant, and in the case of tribes in Northeast India, this sector predominantly comprises government employment and informal employment in the private sector. In the latter, employment is generally contractual, salary/wages are low, and working conditions are bad and unsafe and demand long hours.

The movement toward the service sector has also led to shifting patterns of residence. Traditionally, tribes lived on agriculture supplemented by forest products and were bound to live in a village. The move to non-agricultural occupations has led to migration from villages to towns, so that in the last two decades there has been a phenomenal rise in the number of tribal people living in towns, which have increased in size and number. This process of urbanisation seems to be connected with the national agenda of decentralising governance. The percentages of tribal peoples living in urban contexts across the Northeast can be seen in the following table.[5]

5. Government of India, "Statistical Profile of Scheduled Tribes."

Northeast State	Percentage of Tribal People in Urban Population
Mizoram	92.5
Nagaland	70.8
Meghalaya	70.4
Arunchal Pradesh	51.0
Manipur	13.4
Assam	5.1
Tripura	5.0

It is clear that the tribal states are experiencing rapid growth in urbanization, but the non-tribal states have also gone through this process. The manner in which urbanization is growing is very haphazard and with little concern for ecology and the environment and inadequate civic amenities such as water, sanitation, and cleanliness, all of which will take a toll on the health of the people.

Education and Health

Notwithstanding the rapid rise of urbanization, economic development seems to be slow and sluggish in the region. However, the social sector seems to be doing relatively well since in the Northeast regions, the number of people living below the poverty line in some of the states is lower than the national average for India. Similar is the case with education and some aspects of health indicators. In 2011, the literacy rate in India was 72.99 percent for the population as a whole, compared to 58.96 percent for the total Indian tribal population. However in relation to these numbers, the literacy rate in tribal states was high, as shown in the following table.[6]

Northeast State	Rates of Literacy in Percentages
Mizoram	91.5
Nagaland	80.0
Meghalaya	74.5
Arunchal Pradesh	64.6
Manipur	77.4
Tripura	79.1
Sikkim	79.7
Assam	72.0

6. Government of India, "Statistical Profile of Scheduled Tribes."

In fact, education is one of the areas in which the tribes have been doing well, which is reflected in enrolment in higher education and the density of higher educational institutions such as colleges and universities. Very few states outside the region enjoy such density, although there are grey areas. One of the most critical is the quality of education in both school education and higher education. Education alone is not enough; what is imperative is quality education. And quality has to begin at the level of schools, especially with basic science education and mathematics.

The pattern is however not the same in some key health indicators. For example, infant mortality in the region, with the exception of Mizoram (57) and Assam (61), has been higher than the national average of 57, and even the tribal average of 62.1. This issue may be due to a lack of access to health care facilities in far-flung areas where a large number of villages still lack roads and means of transport. However, in mortality rates for under-five-year-old children, tribal people in the region are better placed in comparison to the national average, except for the states of Arunachal Pradesh (104) and Meghalaya (119). The national average of under-fives mortality has been 74.3 for India and 95.7 for the tribal population as a whole.[7] While this number is a positive sign, it is also a fact that tribal communities are deeply impacted by other health problems including substance abuse (alcohol and drugs), HIV/AIDS, and cancer. Equally important have been the mental health issues following the protracted phase of violence and armed conflicts in the region. These are not merely individual problems but have implications for families and communities. Further, if mental health issues are widespread, they are a problem for the community.

Unemployment and Migration

As observed earlier, social development indicators are relatively better among the tribes of Northeast India compared to tribal peoples in other parts of the country, especially with regard to education. As a result of high literacy rates, a large number of people have moved to higher education. Until the early 1990s or so, the educated did not have to struggle much for jobs in the region as the newly formed states could accommodate them. However with the downsizing of government jobs as a part of structural adjustment programmes, the state employment sector has shrunk. What was known as class IV and class III employment has almost disappeared from the scene so that the state,

7. Government of India, "Statistical Profile of Scheduled Tribes." All figures are out of 1,000 live births.

the key provider of jobs, no longer has space for the educated or uneducated unemployed. At the same time, a large-scale job-providing private sector, either in manufacturing or services, is almost non-existent in the region. In fact, the manufacturing sector has historically been weak resulting, as we have seen, in the important provider of jobs, other than agriculture, being the service sector. However, even here it was the state employment that really mattered. So service sector employment is primarily confined to the private sector. But in the Northeast such employment is predominantly unorganized, informal, low wage/salary, and without security of any kind. Thus, neither the manufacturing sector nor the service sector in the region are able to generate the scale and kinds of employment needed, which results in people being forced to migrate outside the region for employment. Whereas earlier migration of people was into the region from outside, today that process has gone into reverse. Not only educated people but also those without higher education qualifications are faced with the unemployment problem and have to move out of the region to seek employment in India's expanding megacities. In short, while the social sector has relatively done well, the economic sector has not been doing well.

Political Pragmatism and Political Culture

One of the key economic problems in the region is its growth rate. In fact, all of the states in the region are deficit states to varying degrees and are heavily dependent on national state grants. Indeed, many of them are dependent on the central government to the extent of over 90 percent, which explains the nature of the alliances which regional political parties tend to build with the national parties. In the process of this pragmatism, all other issues such as values, ideology, and the consequences that such alliances are likely to have in society in general, and their areas and communities in particular, are not seriously considered and deliberated upon. Alliance with the Bharatiya Janata Party (BJP) in recent years is a case in point.[8] The ideology and imagination of India promoted by this party is in striking contrast to the way the people of the Northeast in general, and tribal people in particular, have articulated their sense of identity and values since India's independence. Indeed, the presence of the BJP in the long run can have unprecedented consequences for the region, especially for tribal societies given the character of the party and the affiliates

8. The Bharatiya Janata Party is the Hindu nationalist party now in government in India under the leadership of Narenda Modi.

it works with. The Rashtriya Swayam Sangh (RSS),[9] its affiliated organization, and organizations sympathetic to its ideology have already made an impact in many states of the region, and these organizations work at almost all levels. Some of the sectors in which they are very active in the region and among the tribes are education, health, and development. It is through these activities that they sow the seeds of their values and ideology, and the alliances with such parties only help these organizations to consolidate their position in the region.

The heavy dependence on state grants or resources has led to other kinds of problems in the region; the most important is the corruption or appropriation of state exchequer meant for the collective good of the community for personal gain. Corruption is one of the endemic problems in the Northeast, even among the tribes. Notwithstanding the impact of such problems on the society, the desire and seriousness to deal with this issue does not seem to exist.

Tribal Customary Practices – Strengths and Weaknesses

Despite social and political transformations, customs and traditions remain strong in certain spheres of tribal society. One such sphere is the ownership and management patterns of land, forest, and other resources. Community ownership either in the form of clan or village provides some safeguards or constraints on the state acquiring land for its projects, including the agenda of converting forests into reserved or other types of state-controlled territory. Such diversion deprives local communities of access to the resources on which they have been dependent for their livelihood and other usages. The traditional system of ownership posed constraints on land grabbing by powerful community members for their personal use, and in many ways such traditional, customary practices remind members of the values of egalitarianism and community bonding. Such patterns of ownership for the tribal people can also act as an alternative way of thinking about development.

At the same time, there is a certain inherent inequity in the systems of traditional ownership and governance in addressing questions of equity and justice. An example is the inequality of women in regard to access to inheritance and participation in the public sphere of life. The need for tribal communities to address the issues of women, such as a share in inheritance and the institutions of governance, in the changing context of society, as these changes that are likely to empower women, both traditional and modern, are being resisted. It is

9. Rashtriya Swayam Sangh is the organization promoting Hindutva, the Hindu nationalist ideology closely associated with the BJP and the government of Narenda Modi.

imperative that these issues be confronted and amicable solutions worked out, which is very much in tune with the values of egalitarianism in traditional tribal society as well as values and principles of modern democratic institutions.

Orality, Folklore, and Myth

Finally, coming to the particular theme of this book, much has been written on tribal society since the colonial period. A considerable body of knowledge exists today which began under colonial rule and administration, and those who produced studies during this phase were mostly scholar-administrators, Christian missionaries, and anthropologists. They were also mostly Europeans and wrote on the tribes from what they observed as outsiders and from the vantage point of their values and perspectives. In this process of producing knowledge, it is likely that they may at times have distorted facts or inadequately presented them. They may have even misinterpreted tribal institutions, values, customs, traditions, and worldviews. Indian scholars and administrators have added knowledge on the tribes, but the question remains: what is the nature and type of knowledge the Indian scholars have added? Have they altogether produced new facts and new knowledge in a sense not touched upon and discussed in the earlier works, or have they built on the works of earlier scholars by supplementing new facts and interpretation? How far have such facts and interpretations reflected social reality as experienced and interpreted by tribes themselves? At the same time, the tribes have undergone change and moved away from some of the critical customs, traditions, and worldviews of their ancestors. To go back and retrieve knowledge of the past prior to possessing the tradition of reading and writing is not easy but is an exercise worth pursuing. This exercise demands a return to the tribal tradition of producing, disseminating, and transmitting knowledge. To this end scholars have to rely on the past storage of knowledge, which means falling back not only on oral traditions such as myths, folklore, stories, legends, and songs, but also on traditional ways, practices, and ideas and the meanings they reflected and symbolized.

2

Unleashing the Power of Orality, Myth, and Folklore

Charles B. Madinger and Rocelyn Anog-Madinger

The HIV/AIDS epidemic was ravaging Northern Nigeria's largest metropolitan areas. It seemed like all the well-intentioned attempts to arrest it fell on deaf ears. People were not connecting the urgency of the crisis to their part of the continent. The death of almost every adult from age twenty-five to fifty in Malawi "was their problem, not ours." How could an intervention message sink in when AIDS was on the same destructive path in Nigeria's cities and villages?

The Hausa people across the north of Nigeria own a rich tradition of music, proverbs, and folktales. A "Show Love and Care"[1] programme drew upon that tradition to compose a song to communicate the dangers of this disease. Attention was also drawn to a key Hausa proverb that resonated with everyone and turned the tide. The song simply changed the words to a famous Hausa tune, using the proverb which says: "Don't wait 'till the grass sticks you in the eye to cut it." The song made an immediate connection because if you wait until the grass is tall in this part of the world, you will end up dead from the bite of a poisonous cobra! A six-hour interactive audio series reached

1. "Show Love and Care" was a programme designed and developed for HIV/AIDS intervention in Nigeria by Voice for Humanity with local Christians and Muslims leading in Plateau and Kano States. The program produced extraordinary results from which emerged the principles we now call the Incarnated Model or the Holistic Model of Orality. These models also drew from similar successful programs in Afghanistan, Iraq and Sudan.

every household in one of the local government areas (LGAs), and the spread of HIV/AIDS in the region was drastically reduced![2]

The arts of myth and folklore serve as tools of communication that enhance the engagement of the hearts and minds of hearers. When appropriately utilized, the impact of a message grows exponentially. First, we move from the oral expressions themselves – myth, folklore, narrative, etc. described in the other chapters in this book – to utilizing the power that drives them to higher and broader impact. The question may now be raised, especially for people from the West: "Do we fully engage that power or continue in the modern status quo?" Nearly all mission training has historically been deeply rooted in Western literate principles and methods, even for people intending to live and work in contexts of very low print-text literacy.

A lexical definition of orality is simply a preference for and reliance upon oral communication. Note, however, that orality is about communication, or learned expression of inner speech.[3] A conceptual definition of orality is how we come to shared meaning through receiving, processing, remembering, and passing on information. An operational definition of orality is a complex of the ways and means through which Jesus communicated. Anthropologists speak of orality in terms of oral tradition cultures and literature.[4] Many educators speak in terms of "oral-learners" in contrast to print/text or literate learners and how each remembers truth and information. Linguists and Bible translators mainly focus on literacy and ever-changing languages.[5] Sociologists relate orality to the ways that communities and societies receive and pass on their values. Artists focus on the creative expressional forms, while communications and media professionals find the appropriate channels for the diffusion of messages through mass media. Finally, some missionaries and churches promote their preferred methodologies of Bible storytelling as orality, but what we wish to call

2. Igho Ofotokun and Charles Madinger, "Murya Agagi: Final Report to USAID on the Show Love and Care program of VFH, " 2005 Unpublished. The programme demonstrated a 26 percent increase in HIV/AIDS literacy which exceeded every other programme in the region.

3. Grant Lovejoy, "The Extent of Orality," *Journal for Baptist Theology and Ministry* 15, no. 1 (2008): 121–34.

4. Elizabeth Tonkin. "Investigating Oral Tradition," *Journal of African History* 27, no. 2 (1986): 203–13.

5. However, note the comment of James A. Maxey when describing a shift in New Testament scholarship which involves the recognition that the New Testament was itself composed "to be heard and experienced in an oral setting" which was "not so different than the oral settings found in places like Africa today." He adds, "The Bible was for the most part created, transmitted, and received in a predominantly oral context. This should affect how we go about Bible translation today." *From Orality to Orality: A New Paradigm for Contextual Translation of the Bible* (Eugene, OR: Cascade, 2009), 1.

kingdom missiologists, evangelists, pastors, and trainers can rethink orality and discover more holistic perspectives for broader applications and deeper impact.

Orality and Communication

Conceptually, orality has to do with how a society or culture receives, processes, remembers, and passes on information and truth. As communication, orality necessarily helps us convey meanings from one to another through the use of mutually understood signs and symbols. Some prefer a high dependence on oral communication, and some lower – and this preference is on a sliding scale. But first, a discussion is necessary on communication in general.

From the beginning, according to the Genesis story, orality is one aspect of what sets us apart from the rest of creation. The Triune God lives in intimate community, communicated together before anything was, and then chose to create human beings in the divine image. God spoke the world into existence, talked directly with our first parents as they walked together in the garden (Gen 3:8–9), and later visited the patriarchs in human form (Gen 18). The great variety of forms of divine communication is seen in visions (Gen 15:1), dreams (Dan 2), writing on tablets of stone (Exod 31:18), writing on a wall with a finger (Dan 5), and in various linguistic forms including riddles (Ezek 17), parables (Ezek 16), and laments (Ezek 19). God commissioned songs (Deut 31:22–32:1–43; Zeph 3:17) and finally spoke with all the elements of human communication through his incarnate Son (Heb 1:1–2). God "spoke" creatively so there would be no question about the meaning of his love and the content of the message.

Orality is our in-the-image-of-God shared characteristic of communication that begins by design in the human brain. We see an image in our mind, and it cries out to be named from our earliest development. We finally express that "inner speech"[6] by verbalizing or signing that image.[7] For example when seeing our mother, we identify her as Ma, Momma, Nanay, Maji, Mor – whatever language we received as a gift to express ourselves as infants. Eventually some learn to express that image in a picture or drawing, or by telling a story about her, creating a poem, then a song, instrumental music, sign language, and the list goes on.

---

6. See Lev Vygotsky, *Mind and Society: The Development of Higher Psychological Processes* (Cambridge: Harvard University Press, 1978).

7. See for example "ASL: 'Mom' and 'Dad,'" LifePrint.com, https://www.lifeprint.com/asl101/pages-signs/m/momdad.htm.

Everyone Is an Oral Learner[8]

Everyone functions out of orality, even if that person cannot hear, audibly speak, or visually see. The inner speech has to find expression, and written text is only one of many mediums. In fact, we can say that literacies are an expression of orality. Every act of literacy begins with inner speech and finds expression through print/text, graphic arts, sign language, braille, and even mathematics. Literacies begin with orality. Reading and writing are just one expression of orality – not something apart from it. So we all come into this world one hundred percent reliant on that orality, and the issue then becomes how we developmentally learn to express our inner speech to form a framework.

Frameworks are ways of viewing the world and interpreting it. In cultural jargon we speak of worldviews; in educational circles we call them schemas; or in leadership terminology we refer to a paradigm. A framework is what helps us to gain knowledge and differentiate our beliefs from other opinions (an epistemology). A framework is how we make sense of our environment and the movements of our lives; frames are both windows on the world and lenses that bring the world into focus. At the same time, they filter out the things we either do not need or want.[9]

The Innsbruck Goggle Experiments conducted by Theodor Erismann and Ivo Kohler developed a set of goggles that inverted the field of human vision.[10] Their goal was to determine how a person might function when everything was "upside down." After about a day fitted with the goggles, Kohler could begin pouring water, determine right from left, and even ride a bicycle. The key was to continuously wear the goggles to reorient the brain to see the world in a new way. Taking them off after adjusting to this inverted world also produced disorientation when returning to what the rest of the world sees as normal. The frameworks of orality are much the same as the perspective of the goggles. People who went to university or seminary learned how to see the world and the Christian mission with greater focus, but the "lenses" they obtained in

8. The term "oral learner" is most frequently used to describe the millions of people belonging to oral cultures; it signifies respect for them and their cultures in contrast to terminology such as "illiterates" which contains negative value judgements on those cultures. See "Making Disciples of Oral Learners (English)," ION: International Orality Network, https://orality.net/content/making-disciples-of-oral-learners-english/.

9. J. David Johnson, "A framework for interaction (FINT) scale: Extensions and refinement in an industrial setting," *Communication* 48, no. 2 (1997): 127–41. https://doi.org/10.1080/10510979709368496.

10. Pierre Sachse, et. al., "The World Is Upside Down: Innsbruck Goggle Experiments Conducted by Theodor Erismann (1883–1961) and Ivo Kohler (1915–1985)," *Cortex* 92 (April 2017): 222–232.

this way will never be worn by audiences in the majority world. The goggles are good, especially when seeing things that go unnoticed without them, but the challenge is to be able to take what has been seen or learned in this way and apply it for people who have never known our equipment, orientation, and skills.

High Orality Reliance (HOR) Framework

Over their first few years of life, many children learn and develop a framework of high orality reliance (HOR), or a high reliance on all that goes into communication in a traditional society. They learn to value processing things together, to operate with a *kairos*[11] perspective of time, and to archive important things in proverbs, stories, songs, and other local arts. Ways of reasoning might be considered random, and they begin repeating a type of processing, following a narrative or story most easily, deeply respecting elders and the past and traditions, listening for the familiar word, "becoming the music" in spontaneous song and dance, and organizing their world in concrete tangible ways.[12]

Low Orality Reliance (LOR) Framework

On the other hand, children who learn within a framework of low orality reliance (LOR), or a low reliance on all that goes into communication, tend to prefer or value processing things individually, operating within a *chronos*[13] perspective of time, archiving important things in writing or documents, and organizing their thoughts in outline form rather than narrative. In such cultures people follow a line of reasoning that might be considered a linear progression of processing, rewarding innovation and youth, clearly defining words and phrases, and organizing their world in principles and abstractions.

11. *Kairos* is a Greek term signifying time at a particular opportune moment for something to happen.

12. For a more complete discussion of the characteristics and tendencies of orality, see "Orality Research," The Institute for Orality Strategies, http://i-ostrat.com/orality. The original psychodynamics were proposed by Walter Ong in *Orality and Literacy: The Technologizing of the Word* (London: Routledge, 2002). See also William Parker, *Cultural and Academic Stress Imposed on Afro-Americans: Implications for Educational Change* (Princeton: E.R.I.C., 1980).

13. *Chronos* is a Greek term referring to the perspective of "chronological progression" of time measured in minutes, hours, days, etc. For example, we meet at a certain hour and minute of the day.

Most individuals who have undergone formal education, and especially those who went on to higher education including seminary training, have lost their original high oral reliance over time and even changed brain functions as a result of developing reading skills.[14] In literate cultures there is a move away from a high dependence on oral communication and a natural progression toward low orality. These people learn more and more means of expressing their inner speech through multiple oralities and literacies. Some learn the literacies of sign language or braille, while others master the literacies of mathematics, accounting, computer software, musical notation, etc. They function well and learn by reading and studying individually and deciphering complex words and abstract puzzles. Education involves listening to lectures with limited interaction with other people, and the enjoyment of music takes place by withdrawing into private worlds, listening alone to recordings. Such people view time in measured increments, teach, make disciples, and archive almost everything for print-text accessibility.

Both frameworks remain with us for life like all other culturally acquired parts of us: the food we eat and drink, the clothes we wear, the language we speak, the music that touches our deepest feelings, and even how we learn and relate to others. We learn and adapt to other preferences, and even appear to have made a shift. Yet the culture we have imbibed early on remains our dominant framework. However, make no mistake, these possibilities do not function rigidly as either/or, oral/literate, or any other dichotomy. They exist on a continuum from HOR to LOR and change over time along that continuum.

We are going to provide an example of shifts and tensions resulting from movements between the two cultural and linguistic spheres just described. A good friend of ours grew up with a very high orality reliance in a small village in Nigeria. He was the first of his family to graduate from secondary school and then went on to a Bible school and seminary. Eventually he rose to a prominent position in his denomination and enrolled in a top American seminary where he earned a PhD in intercultural studies. This history sounds as though he made a polar shift from one end of the spectrum to the other. However for many of his course exams as well as for his qualifying examination, he pleaded to be allowed an oral test instead of the normal written paper. He explained that he always reverts back to his roots when thinking something through, and speaking about what he had learned had much higher value because, as he explained "You are what you say, not what you write. It's who I am."

14. Dehaence Stanislas, Pegado Felipe, and Braga Lucias, "How learning to read changes the cortical network for vision and language," *Science Express* (November 2010): 1–10.

LOR Framework Domination

Some things just need an LOR medium. Moses gave the books of the law that were written by God himself on tablets of stone, giving permanence to his spoken word for all generations. That written word, however, was first in the mind of God, then spoken. After recording it in a textual form, God expected it to be spoken, listened to, even sung (Deut 32:44). Over time this gift of God of a text extension of inner speech somehow began to bear more weight than the message itself. Jewish rabbis and elders made meaning out of each letter of a word, and invented meaning and applications by their own design for keeping the law. The text became more important than the one who had spoken the message, and what he had intended to convey became lost in abstract speculations.

Much later, when the Bible was translated and eventually printed in book form, and the kingdom of God expanded into what we now call Europe, people with the ability to read, write, and explain the word in abstractions and principles came into prominence. At the same time leaders recognized that the overwhelming majority of humanity did not read or reason in that way, as witnessed for example by the importance of icons (visual images) in Eastern Orthodoxy, and the Roman Catholic use of the rosary and stained glass windows functioning as memory tools in cathedrals and churches.

With Gutenberg's invention of the printing press and the later era of the Enlightenment, universities emerged to provide education for a literate elite whose learning made them respected and powerful. Colonialism spread those values around the world, suppressing the oral cultures and their frameworks in an effort to make them more "civilized."[15] What has been called "The Great Century" of Protestant missions[16] witnessed waves of passionate, self-sacrificing missionaries taking the Christian message to peoples in Africa, Asia, and Latin America and teaching indigenous people how to read and write, often in the languages of the colonialists.

The converts were quick learners, mastering the languages and the ways and means of communication, educational systems, and commerce. Western missions regarded the provision of education as a key component of their task, but this created tensions and resistance within tribal societies since local leaders

---

15. Jack Goody, *The Domestication of the Savage Mind* (Cambridge: Cambridge University Press, 1977).

16. The phrase comes from the title of Kenneth Scott Latourette's *History of the Expansion of Christianity: Vol 4: The Great Century in Europe and the United States of America* (New York: Harper, 1941).

feared that what was taught in mission schools posed a threat to the very foundations of traditional cultures. Over time, Bible colleges and universities emerged granting degrees and the prestige that accompanied new knowledge and prestigious titles. The colonial missionaries freely gave what they had to those in need of new tools, but these tools came with unintended consequences: their teaching, preaching, evangelism, and leadership development all came through the lenses of low orality reliance. Western missions unintentionally overrode the new disciples' preference for high orality reliance and attempted to impose another framework which the converts in their turn frequently adopted, often living in two separate worlds. The dominant voices accompanying colonial power drowned out the voices of those they came to serve.

This approach perpetuated the LOR paradigm that came to permeate modern Christian missions regardless of what they may look like on the outside. For example, training programmes in church planting among tribal peoples may appear to take local cultures seriously. Yet frequently they make use of Western practices and imported materials which instruct participants in methods of preaching propositional, bullet-pointed sermons which ignore the reality of audiences composed of traditional people who process the word collectively. Missions and denominations offer leadership training, evangelism presentations, and Bible school and seminary courses organized around principles and outlines originating in the modern Western context, and the cycle goes on unbroken.

Further, the overwhelming majority of Christian curricula originate from very LOR designers (just the use of these terms should sound an alarm). Even when Bible stories are involved, and despite a recognition that they originate in HOR contexts, they are related and applied in ways which reflect the communicator's LOR assumptions and methods. Radio and other media are often simply LOR messages recorded and broadcast with the assumption that the orality gap has been bridged.[17]

The fundamental cause of this situation is that people from highly literate cultures become so oriented by their LOR goggles that they do not see the world in the same ways as the oral majority.[18] To work within this oral majority is not a matter of merely adopting a few oral methods, however valid such

17. The orality gap is the difference between where LOR leaders can teach, preach, and serve and the level of orality reliance of those we consider the oral majority. See Madinger C., 'Applications of the Orality Discussion' *Evangelical Missions Quarterly*, 53/1: 54–59.

18. Dawn Herzog Jewell, "Winning the oral majority," *Christianity Today* 50, no. 3 (2006): 56.

methods might be, such as using song, drama, proverbs, parables, stories, media, etc. What is imperative is *the removal of the LOR goggles as a condition of experiencing the world of the other, and recognising the power of orality to enable communication which touches the hearts of peoples in HOR societies, and in the process exposes the limitations of the Western shaping of the gospel.*

An Operational Definition: The Incarnated Model

Jesus confronted the Jewish elite with the message his Father commanded him to speak (John 12:48–49). Our point is that communication exponentially impacts an audience to the degree that we follow the example set by Christ. Using the principles of orality does not guarantee transformation, but the neglect of those principles absolutely inhibits more thorough transformation. If God in Christ intentionally framed his communication in ways and means that bring the highest impact, we must rethink how we communicate.

As we noted earlier, God exists in three persons communicating with each other, speaking the world into existence, and then communicating multimodally with humankind throughout history. His inner speech designed the universe and resulted in our being. His expressions of that divine inner speech shout out in creation ("The heavens declare the glory of God," Ps 19:1), and his interactions throughout human history have poured out that inner speech in revelation after revelation. How does that communication relate to myth, folklore, and other arts? They are part of God's model. Luke records how Jesus grew up and lived within a culture that was overwhelmingly oral, and he taught in ways that reflected the forms of communication used in that context. Consider his unique parables, examples of storytelling which involved immense skill and impacted his hearers then and continue to resonate in widely different cultural settings even now. Or take a specific example in the scene of a dinner in the home of Simon the Pharisee (Luke 7:36–50). Jesus lived in the region as a Galilean Jew and knew all the nuances of that culture. So when he ate at Simon's dinner party, he did it in a reclining position, leaning on one arm (v. 36). He recognized the impropriety of allowing a woman to touch him as she did, especially one known as a "sinful" woman (v. 37). He spoke and listened in the language(s) common to the region and used the terms everyone around the table understood and even expected. When finally confronting Simon the Pharisee, Jesus used specific terms that struck at the heart of every Jew in their mother tongue (vv. 44–46). The brief parable about debts owed to a moneylender mirrors the social life of the time, both the crippling problems of debt and the existence of wealthy people who profited from the suffering and poverty of the poor. Jesus made cultural references to the kiss of greeting (withheld by the host) and the "water for my feet" insultingly not offered, and then gave his controversial declaration of how sins could be forgiven (vv. 44–46).

Note that Jesus did all of this in the home of a Pharisee. No accident. The medium was a fairly small group of locally influential people. Jesus repeated this message for this kind of place and with the right number of people to guarantee that the message would be unmistakably received: "I have the power to forgive sins." He gave the same message in other homes (Matt 9:1–5) and even in the temple courts (John 8:1–11). But he chose small groups (micromedia), and often spoke in the homes of people including Peter, Matthew, Mary and Martha, Lazarus, and Zacchaeus. The wealthy Pharisee maybe had twenty or thirty dinner guests in his house for the occasion of a debate with a rabbi. Jesus penetrated the religious networks like Simon's circle of friends in his home and at other times in temple discussions (Luke 2:46), private meetings (John 3), and dinners like this one. By doing so, Jesus ensured that his kingdom message would go viral throughout their ranks. He eventually confronted Simon about the forgiveness God wants to grant that is based on love, not law. Nestled in the story is the tenderness and all-out commitment of a "sinful woman" who spared no expense to honour Jesus as her Saviour and King. She brought with her a product of one of the specialized arts of her day – perfuming (v. 37) – which bombarded the senses with a fragrance reserved only for the wealthy. Some entrepreneur had concocted an exotic mixture of expensive spices, blended the oils, and then sealed the mixture in an alabaster jar, a translucent vase that was an artwork in itself. What this woman did impacted the guests in a way that meant they could not help but repeat the story over and over. To make the event memorable for Simon, Jesus used a proverb: "But whoever has been forgiven little loves little" (Luke 7:47).

We contend that the use of the arts discussed in this book – myth and folklore in this context – reflects the communication patterns of God as reflected in the mission he commanded his Son to fulfil. Therefore when we as his children use these arts, they increase the possibility of transformational impact among higher orality reliant peoples. The point is this: when we use the same principles and methods that God chose to use to communicate his message, we choose his transformational design for deeper impact.

Implications of Orality

Unleash more of the power intended by God for human communication. Think of preaching and teaching as sources of water. When we teach and preach without using LOR principles and methods, we restrict the amount of water others can access. How can we supply the most living water? Organize thoughts, teachings, and theologies in narrative forms, and harness the power of the group. The word of God was never for mere personal consumption, reflection, and application but is meant for community. Package the message through arts, and rethink orality theology and theory. This practice is not rocket science, but neither is it simply intuitive. First, orality as a discipline is new to the Western cultural context of the Enlightenment, but leaders throughout history have understood its power. As mentioned earlier, the Orthodox Christians of the East have always understood the power of visual images, while Roman Catholics taught people how to pray with rosaries and in oral cultures present the gospel message visually through stained glass windows and murals. The Protestant Reformers produced new music and liturgies, and although the invention of printing resulted in increasingly literate cultures, Martin Luther's translation of the Bible into German highlighted the importance of mother-tongues and led to all peoples being able to say "God speaks our language."

In our educational experiences, from sophisticated urban seminaries to "under a tree" grassroots training, who taught us or modelled the principles of orality? Who used these principles in the classrooms we sat in? How we learn, the discipline of "memory," can go beyond telling us what we need to know. How we teach can lead students to discover "new knowledge" through adult learning models using the power of narrative.[19] The difference is "in-forming" versus "trans-forming." Dedicating more effort to transmitting the message on the wavelengths people prefer to listen to and learn on is as important as what we attempt to communicate. Learning to go beyond our acquired ways and means of communication poses a steep learning curve, and some never consider it, while others deem it too overwhelming.

Christians should be encouraged to integrate the descriptive disciplines modelled by Jesus as a synergistic whole. Remember, orality is a framework – a schema, a total system that works together. Neglecting any one aspect decreases impact, but using the whole system multiplies impact. These disciplines also relate to professional or academic practices: culture including anthropology

19. Malcomb Knowles, Holton Elwood, Richard Swanson, *The Adult Learner* (New York: Routledge, 2015); Jerome Bruner, *Actual Minds, Possible Worlds* (Boston: Harvard University Press, 1987).

and especially worldview; language and linguistics; literacies such as reading, writing, comprehension, numeracies, and signs; networks, especially the path a message takes to go farthest the fastest; memory including appropriate mnemonic devices, learning theories, and long and short term memory; the arts that package the message to touch the heart by engaging all the senses; and media such as mass, collective, small, social, and digital. All lead to the highest form of communication – "inter-personal" with the Living Word. Jesus deemed it necessary to use all of these disciplines so that we might know him. How can we not follow his example?

We need to rethink what and how we publish. The publishing world is changing at warp speed. YouTube, Facebook, websites, and blogs have changed the landscape forever. We seem to be moving to much higher orality reliant formats that require fewer words and more video, audio, and graphic communication. Publications, even as good as this one, will have to adapt. You are reading our inner speech, yet we could be communicating more with you using higher orality reliant principles and methods. Soon digi-books with introductory videos, sign language or other media will be the norm. Hyperlinks may replace footnotes. Authors will likely do more self-publishing of living, breathing, interactive publications in which "readers" can react and authors immediately edit and revise, and to which consumers from anywhere in the world can have direct access with a simple online search at little or no financial expense.

Present-day formal and non-formal educators struggle to teach and model higher orality reliance principles and methods. From Bible schools in rural Kenya to house churches in China, teaching models that originated in the West remain strongly *low* orality reliant. In most higher education, the Enlightenment idealization of textuality, literacy, and reading still dominates communication and education models and devalues all we associate with orality. This means we need to build HOR training paradigms like oral Bible schools and training organizations that capitalize on the arts. Some churches are doing so among the emerging digit-oral generations, but more work is needed.[20] How about oral Bible schools that teach a narrative theology delivered through Bible narratives and grounded texts, songs, and regional wisdom "oral" literature?[21]

---

20. See Samuel Chiang, *Beyond Western Literate Practices: Continuing Conversations in Orality and Theological Education* (Hong Kong: Condeo, 2014).

21. See Ruth Finnegan, "Orality and literacy: Epic heroes of human destiny?" *International Journal of Learning* 10 (2003): 1551–60.

We can discover the path back to the power of orality. The discussions of myth and folktales which make up the bulk of this book demonstrate the crucial importance of these forms of communication in Northeast India and will help us build stronger foundations of communicating truth so that we can multiply the work of others in this area. God will bless the work of our hands when that work is called into existence through fervent prayer, using his design, and completed by his power through his servants for his glory. He preserved his thoughts and expressions for all time, until time shall be no more, through the art of textual expression *so that* it could be *heard* and sensorially experienced throughout all generations as a witness to his great and glorious deeds.

> I will open my mouth with a parable;
>   I will utter hidden things, things from of old –
> things we have heard and known,
>   things our ancestors have told us.
> We will not hide them from their descendants;
>   we will tell the next generation
> the praiseworthy deeds of the LORD,
>   his power, and the wonders he has done.
> He decreed statutes for Jacob
>   and established the law in Israel,
> which he commanded our ancestors
>   to teach their children,
> so the next generation would know them,
>   even the children yet to be born,
>   and they in turn would tell their children.
> Then they would put their trust in God
>   and would not forget his deeds
>   but would keep his commands. (Ps 78:2–7)

For further information on this subject, see the following:

Charles Madinger, "Coming to terms with orality," *Missiology* 38, no. 2 (2010): 201–13.

Charles Madinger, "A literate's guide to the oral galaxy," *Orality Journal* 2, no. 2 (2013): 14–40.

3

West African Insights on Ethnic Identity, Myth, and Sacred Time

James R. Krabill

For a period of six years, from 1982 to 1988, I lived along with my wife and small children among the Dida people of south central Côte d'Ivoire. Our work in the region was part of a larger initiative undertaken since 1959 by our supporting agency, the North American-based Mennonite Board of Missions, now Mennonite Mission Network, of establishing fraternal relationships with a variety of independent religious movements across West Africa.[1]

The Dida are one of sixty ethnic groups in this former French colony and are situated geographically and linguistically in the larger Kru family of peoples scattered across the southwest region of the country. Twenty-some languages are spoken within the Kru grouping alone, languages which are by no means inter-intelligible, though speakers seem to recognize the existence of certain connections and common cultural relationships.[2]

1. The nature and early history of these relationships are described by Edwin and Irene Weaver in *The Uyo Story* (Elkhart, IN: Mennonite Board of Missions, 1970) and *From Kuku Hill* (Elkhart, IN: Institute of Mennonite Studies, 1975). See also Wilbert R. Shenk, "Mission Agency and African Independent Churches," *International Review of Missions* 63, no. 251 (October 1974): 475–91; David A. Shank, "A Survey of American Mennonite Ministries to African Independent Churches," *Mission Focus* 13, no. 1 (March 1985): 1–5; David A. Shank, "Mission Relations with the Independent Churches of Africa," *Missiology* 13, no. 1 (January 1985): 24–44.

2. Much of the research data in this essay was the focus of my 1989 doctoral dissertation and can be found in published form under the title, *The Hymnody of the Harrist Church among the Dida of South-Central Ivory Coast, 1913–1949* (Frankfurt am Main: Peter Lang GmbH [*Studies in the Intercultural History of Christianity* 74], 1995).

Dida Ethnic Identity and Consciousness

In his important 1969 work on Dida social organization, Emmanuel Terray asks the question, "Does there exist, in reality, an ethnic group we can call 'Dida'?" He then proceeds to examine the issue from seven different angles.[3] Twenty pages later, having gleaned what evidence is available from "Dida" history, language, material culture and living patterns, social organization, worldview, centralized institutions, and degree of ethnic consciousness, Terray concludes that

> if one adopts a definition of "ethnic group" which is comprehensive in scope, then the Dida would certainly not constitute such a group. We have seen that the definition of "ethnic group" given by Fortes [i.e., "a group whose component parts have more in common between them than these parts have with those of neighboring groups"] does not permit us to clearly distinguish the Dida from certain of their neighbors. . . . To the contrary, the Western forest region of Ivory Coast from Divo [a Dida urban center] to Daloa [a city among the neighboring Bete people] appears to be a "continuous milieu" where one moves from one zone to another, from one culture to another, from one ethnic group to another with little more than insignificant transitions and arbitrary frontiers. This "continuous milieu" is composed of a constellation of small, sovereign communities made up of all the communities surrounding this center.[4]

It is far beyond the scope of this chapter to fully investigate how and why, given the above information, today's Dida people(s) have come to consider themselves above all as "Dida" and not as something else. We may finally be brought back to the conclusions of certain scholars who have studied other groups in other places and conclude simply that "The tribe is a social unit whose members affirm that they form a social unit,"[5] and "We are sometimes forced to admit, lacking anything better, that a given group exists in reality as little more than what its members consider it to be."[6]

---

3. Emmanuel Terray, "L'organisation sociale des dida de Côte d'Ivoire," *Annales de l'Université d'Abidjan, Series F / Ethnosociologie* 1, no. 2 (1969): 24–25.

4. Terray, "L'organisation sociale" (1969): 35.

5. S. F. Nadel, *A Black Byzantium: The Kingdom of Nupe in Nigeria* (Oxford: Oxford University Press, 1947), 17.

6. J. Richard-Molard, quoted in Paul Mercier, *Tradition, changement, histoire: Les "Somba" du Dahomey Septentrional* (Paris: Editions Anthropos, 1968), 70.

Dida Four Divisions of Time

To comprehend the concept of "myth" among the Dida, it is helpful to understand their concept of "time." People of Eurocentric cultures have grown accustomed to thinking of time divisions in abstract mathematical terms. Thus the average year, we are told, is composed of 365.24220 days, and in the average month, we should expect 29 days, 44 minutes, and 2.8 seconds.

When Africans reckon time, however, writes John Mbiti,

> it is for a concrete and specific purpose, in connection with events but not just for the sake of mathematics. Since time is a composition of events, people cannot and do not reckon it in a vacuum. . . . Instead of numerical calendars there are what one could call phenomenon calendars [e.g., "sunrise," "hunting month," "hot season," "the year of the heavy rains," etc.]. . . . The day, the month, the year, one's life time of human history, are all divided up or reckoned according to their specific events, for it is these that make them meaningful.[7]

The specific events which constitute the traditional Dida "phenomenon calendar" can be grouped into four major time divisions, beginning with the present time and moving back into history and beyond:[8]

1. Time of Nature. In the traditional Dida view of things, there are three "natural events" which keep reoccurring with relentless regularity – the daily rising and setting of the sun, the monthly waxing and waning of the moon, and the yearly appearing of four alternating rainy and dry seasons. There is, most notably, nothing in nature's cycles to indicate how many days should constitute a "week." And in fact, according to Daniel Boorstin, people around the world have found no less than fifteen different ways, for example in bunches of five to ten days each, of arranging their days into the "artificial time

7. John S. Mbiti, *African Religions and Philosophy* (Praeger 1969; reprint Garden City, NY: Anchor Books, 1970), 24–25.

8. A more thorough explanation of these four divisions of time is provided in my unpublished master's thesis, "La tradition orale comme source d'histoire: Quatre problèmes particuliers," Institut Catholique de l'Afrique de l'Ouest / Faculté de Théologie, Abidjan, Ivory Coast, 1979, 109. In that work I identify the four divisions of time or époques as "ecological," "structural," "ancestral," and "mythical."

clusters" we call weeks.[9] Among the Dida, that clustering of time produced a week of six days.

2. Time of Settlement. The year is the longest of nature's cycles. "Decades" and "centuries" are artificial, mathematically produced constructs and don't exist as identifiable time periods in Dida traditional society. To extend time into the past, one can, however, employ phrases like "in my time" (living memory of the present generation), "in my father's time" (one generation back), or "in the time of the grandfathers" (two or more generations back). Another expression – *godo-godo* – is sometimes used to refer to a time in the distant past known today only because previous generations passed on traditions about it. As we work our way backward out of living memory, however, we do encounter one particular event common in most local oral histories, a memory of having picked up and left one or several localities to roam about and finally settle into the present-day village location. My research in the mid-1980s into local, extended family histories among the southern Dida indicates a settlement in their current village localities sometime around or a bit before the turn of the nineteenth century.

3. Time of Migrations. Most Dida have at least this in common: they virtually all claim to have originally come from some place other than where they are presently located. This does not mean, however, that the Dida people as a whole share a common past. Rarely, in fact, do inhabitants of a given region or even of a single village claim common origins. Rather, the unity of residence is often formed from segments of disparate lineages coming from a variety of places. The central location in Ivory Coast of today's Dida populations places them at the very crossroads of both numerous and extremely diverse cultural influences – some, reportedly from western regions, some from the east, and still others from the north. How long people migrated to settle in their current locations is unknown, but likely multiple generations spread across "decades" or even "centuries" of time.

4. Time of Origins. We have referenced thus far three divisions of time among the Dida, beginning with the well-known daily, monthly, and

9. Daniel J. Boorstin, *The Discoverers: A History of Man's Search to Know His World and Himself* (New York: Random House, 1983; reprint New York: Vintage Books, 1985), 13.

yearly cycles of nature, moving back via family histories to a time of settlement, and on into a semi-legendary period of migration. In so doing, we have been edging ever closer to a time when "time" as such did not exist because, as Noss puts it, "there are no landmarks to which events in time remain attached in people's memories."[10] In stepping out of the "time of migrations" into the "time of origins," we are stepping out of "history" and into the remote primeval period when the world and human life first came to be.

Sacred Time, Myths, and Didactic Narratives

We of course never truly "step out" of history and into the time of primeval beginnings, for creation myths are often aetiological in nature and attempt to explain certain current historical sociocultural realities (e.g., wars, migrations, epidemics, etc.) and to justify in general how things in the present came to be the way they are.[11]

Oral tradition scholar Jan Vansina refers to oral materials found in this fourth time division as "didactic narratives" whose primary purpose is to instruct. These narratives, he says,

> attempt to explain the world, culture and society. When this explanation is given by making reference to some kind of religious origins, then these are called myths. If, on the other hand, the explanation is in no way religious, then we have an aetiological narrative. . . . In most cases, myths do not intend to describe events having taken place in the past, but rather in a Sacred Time, situated over and above or parallel to profane time. . . . [Myths] contain very few historical elements worthy of faith, except for sporadic bits of information referring to certain archaic situations. In such instances, this type of information is generally very good. But since myths are most often constructed in order to give aetiological explanations, one must be particularly aware of the presence of possible anachronisms.[12]

---

10. Philip A. Noss, "The Oral Story and Bible Translation," *The Bible Translator* 32, no. 3 (July 1981): 301–18.

11. See Louis-Vincent Thomas and René Luneau, *Les religions d'Afrique noire: Textes et traditions sacrés, vol. 1* (Fayard, 1969; reprint Paris: Editions Stock, 1981), 199, esp. note 18.

12. Jan Vansina, *De la tradition orale: Essai de méthode historique* (Tervuren, Belgium: Musée Royal de l'Afrique Centrale / Annales, Sciences Humaines, 36, 1961), 131–32.

In his important 1969 work on the various components making up the world's religious systems, Ninian Smart identifies seven "dimensions" to be considered. These include the following, in Smart's order: (1) the doctrinal or philosophical; (2) the ritual; (3) the mythic or narrative; (4) the experiential and emotional; (5) the ethical and legal; (6) the social; and (7) the material.[13] One particular challenge of using the term "myth" to title a category is the perception of many people that mythical accounts are made up and not true. Even Smart recognizes this potential conflict for members of Christian faith communities as well as for Jews and Muslims.[14]

The dominant understanding of contemporary mythographers lends little importance to either the veracity or historicity of a myth for it to operate and serve societal purposes. This view is nuanced a bit in the definition offered by Ian Barbour in *Myths, Models and Paradigms*, in which he states that "a myth is in principle neither true nor false, but a useful fiction."[15] Scott Moreau adds a slightly different slant on the "truthfulness" of a given myth by describing it as "any real or fictional story, recurring theme, or character type that appeals to the consciousness of a people by embodying its cultural ideals or by giving expression to deep, commonly held beliefs and felt emotions."[16] Elsewhere in his exploration of religion's "mythic dimension," Moreau explores six paradigms or themes which often appear in myths – themes like "adventure or the quest," "brokenness and redemption," "suffering and sacrifice," "coming of age," "heroism," and "love."[17]

Dida Origin Myths in "Sacred Time"

In contrast to parallel stories found elsewhere in Africa,[18] Dida accounts of the primeval period are relatively few in number and somewhat lacking in detail. "God," known by various names among the Dida, but primarily

13. Ninian Smart, *Dimensions of the Sacred: An Anatomy of the World's Beliefs* (Berkeley: University of California Press, 1996).

14. Smart, *Dimensions*, 130–31.

15. Ian G. Barbour, *Myths, Models and Paradigms: A Comparative Study in Science and Religion* (New York: Harper & Row, 1974), 24.

16. A. Scott Moreau, *Contextualizing the Faith: A Holistic Approach* (Grand Rapids, MI: Baker Academic, 2018), 101.

17. Moreau, *Contextualizing*, 106–9.

18. See Ulli Beier, *The Origin of Life and Death* (London: Heinemann, 1966); Geoffrey Parrinder, *African Mythology* (London: Paul Hamlyn, 1967); and Thomas and Luneau, *Les religions, vol. 1*, 101–57.

as Laago-Lafli, is held to be the creator of the universe and begetter of all humankind. "Humankind" is limited, according to Dja Daniel Beugré,[19] to the only human beings known to the Dida in primeval times, namely the Dida people themselves.

How the first Dida man and woman were created is nowhere described in the mythical narratives that I encountered. According to Beugré, Dida myths "present Man to us in total and complete form as a finished product."[20] For the Djiboua subset of the Dida people living in and around the city of Divo, the first man, named Gnama, simply descended from the heavens, making his premier appearance on earth near the modern-day city of Sassandra in south central Ivory Coast.[21] Another creation version, which will be recounted shortly, suggests that the earliest Dida ancestors were present as witnesses to the formation of the universe as we know it today.

Of more apparent importance for the Dida than the how, when, and where of creation is the relationship of trust and close communion which is said to have existed between Laago-Lafli and the founding ancestor of the Dida people. The precise name of this ancestor is unknown, but it was to this ancestor that God assigned the enormous task of giving life and structure to the Dida people, of creating their customs and traditions, formulating their laws and taboos, inventing their language, and, as Dida Roman Catholic Fr. Egny states, "forever making known the name of God." Not only "making it known," however, but also finding in the first place a name for God that was suitable and worthy of "the One who no living person has ever seen and from whom they have never heard." Writes Egny, "The Name that the Dida venerate and fear, Laago-Lafli, is considered thus by the tradition as the fruit of [the Ancestor's] long meditations and observations, or better yet, as a 'sudden illumination' made to the Ancestor by 'Him upon whom Man wholly depends.'"[22]

How then did it happen, we might well wonder, that the Dida people, with the ancestor forever at their head, slip away from this rather intimate

19. Dja Daniel Beugré, "Les religions didas," unpublished mémoire (No. 220) presented at the Ecole pratique des Hautes Etudes, Section 7, Paris, 1968, 76.

20. Beugré, "Les religions," 50.

21. Gnéba Jacob Akpalé, *L'éducation traditionnelle dida face à l'acculturation*, Université René Descartes, Sciences humaines, Paris 5-Sorbonne / UER: Des sciences de l'éducation), unpublished doctoral dissertation (3ème cycle ès-lettres), 1978, 45–46.

22. Lévry Daniel Egny, *Le monde de l'ancêtre en pays dida: Sa position fâce au Dieu qui vient en Jésus-Christ*, Université des sciences humaines de Strasbourg, Faculté de Théologie Catholique, unpublished doctoral dissertation (these de 3ème cycle), 1978, i-ii. For more detail on the relationship between Laago-Lafli and the first Dida ancestor, see Egny in this same study, i–viii and 174–93.

relationship with Laago-Lafli into a situation of separation and broken communication? Dida myths from this early time of origins do not provide us with abundant details. But there do exist at least three creational accounts which are instructive in explaining how things in the original Dida universe went awry.

> ACCOUNT 1
>
> In the beginning, God created the earth and the sky. The sky was down here, and God lived among men; the earth was up above. But the presence of the earth above soiled the sky and men's food with dirt. Every slight puff of wind filled men's eyes with filth and dust, and so they began complaining to God. When God could tolerate their incessant haranguing no longer, He decided to take leave of men. And this is how everything was turned around. For when God left men, He took the sky with Him and the earth then passed down here below.[23]
>
> ACCOUNT 2
>
> Back at the beginning of time, the sky was very close to the earth, so much so that men were forced to walk around in a bent-over position in order to avoid bumping their heads. One evening a woman was pounding plantain banana foutou in her mortar when she raised her pestle too high in the air and inadvertently poked God in the eye. When this happened, God was so furious that He picked up and went off to a distant place far, far away from the earth.[24]
>
> ACCOUNT 3
>
> After God left and went away, the Dida tried everything to reconnect with God. We sacrificed animals for appeasement. We sent messages through our departed ancestors and other spirits. One woman even got the idea that if she could just go and talk to God, she would be able to settle this matter and put things back in their proper place.

23. Beugré, *Les religions*, 77.

24. Research findings among the elders of a group of Bible students in the village of Yocoboué, 12 October 1982.

> And so the woman fetched a large mortar-bowl, turned it upside down, and planted it firmly in the middle of her courtyard. Then she climbed up on top of it with the hope of reaching the heavens. But, alas, she discovered, the heavens were now too far away.
>
> Not to be discouraged, the woman went around to all the neighboring courtyards and asked to borrow their mortar-bowls. When she had collected all she could find, she stacked them up, one on top of the other, until she had a gigantic pile reaching high into the heavens. Carefully, the woman climbed to the top of the pile, only to discover to her great disappointment, that she was still one mortar short – just one short – of achieving her goal.
>
> What to do? She climbed back down, looked at the pile, and said to herself, "I only need one more mortar. If I just slip one of these out from the bottom of the pile and place it very quickly at the top, I will have exactly what I need." And so, the woman gave it a try and . . . the entire pile came crashing down.[25]

It is far beyond the scope and interests of this chapter to determine the origins of these narratives. Stith Thompson furthermore contends that to even try would be a useless exercise. He writes,

> The origin of all folk tales and myths remains a mystery, just as the origin of language is a mystery. There is of course nothing mystical about it: it is merely impossible to recapture the needed facts. And in the absence of facts, I would wish to leave the ultimate origin of any tale or myth with a large question mark, rather than with a dubious answer.[26]

What we do know is that myths of "paradise lost" similar to these Dida ones have been found in many parts of Africa. Though details may vary, the primary purpose of such stories remains the same: to make a statement about the nature of the present human condition and thereby to explain "the origin

25. Interview in the village of Yocoboué with Papa Robert Sako Dodji, 17 February 1984. This account also appears in published form in James R. Krabill, *Is It Insensitive to Share Your Faith?* (Intercourse, PA: Good Books, 2005), 91–92.

26. Stith Thompson, quoted in Isidore Okpewho, "Rethinking Myth," in *African Literature Today, No. 11: Myth and History*, ed. Eldred Durosimi Jones (London, Ibadan, Nairobi: Heinemann, 1980), 6.

of suffering, illness, death, and separation from God in terms of a sky/earth polarity."[27]

"Is it any wonder that we believed the Prophet Harris?"

When my old friend in the village of Yocoboué, Papa Robert Dodji Sako, finished telling me the story of the woman who tried reaching God by climbing a pile of mortars, he slapped his knee and began to laugh until tears flowed down his cheeks. Then, wiping his face, he leaned forward with renewed vigour and said, "That's what made the message of Harris so powerful! It was Harris who told us that our ancestors had gotten the story only partly right. Maybe it was out of ignorance. More likely out of shame. For whatever reasons, when our ancestors offended God, they ran and hid in the forest behind the trees. It was not God who hid from our ancestors. God actually came looking for them to make things right. If there is no peace with God, Harris told us, it is not God's fault; it is our fault. God has tried everything to get through to us, even sending his son Jesus to show us the way." Then pausing for a moment, Papa Dogui looked at me and asked, "Is it any wonder that when we heard these words, we agreed to give up our objects of worship and receive baptism at the hand of Harris?"[28]

The Prophet Harris? Who was this man? Where did he come from? And what was he doing in Ivory Coast? His remarkable ministry has been recounted in other places and takes us far beyond the scope of this chapter.[29] But keeping it short and simple, we will summarize his story.

As a fifty-three-year-old West African prophet-evangelist, William Wade Harris left his native Liberia and stepped across the French colonial border into neighbouring Côte d'Ivoire in July of 1913. He walked barefoot from village to village for hundreds of miles along the coast, challenging people everywhere to lay aside their traditional objects of worship and turn instead to the one true God. The people Harris encountered had very little if any exposure to the Christian faith prior to his arrival. So building on stories they

27. Benjamin C. Ray, *African Religions: Symbol, Ritual, and Community*, Studies in Religion (Englewood Cliffs, NJ: Prentice-Hall, 1976), 32.

28. Interview with Papa Dodji, 17 February 1984. See also Krabill, *Is It Insensitive*, 92–93.

29. Sources on the life and ministry of William Wade Harris include Gordon Mackay Haliburton, *The Prophet Harris: A Study of an African Prophet and His Mass Movement in the Ivory Coast and the Gold Coast, 1913–1915* (London: Longman, 1971); David A. Shank, *Prophet Harris, the "Black Elijah" of West Africa* (Leiden: Brill, 1994); and my doctoral dissertation cited in note 2 above.

had inherited from their ancestors, Harris challenged his audiences to renew their relationship with God and accept the peace being offered them by the One who had created them in the first place. Harris' ministry lasted a mere eighteen months. But during that brief time an estimated one hundred to two hundred thousand people from over a dozen different ethnic groups, including the Dida, accepted the evangelist's call, received baptism, and took their first steps in their new life in Christ.

How do we account for the amazing success of the Prophet Harris in such a short time? Some attribute it to his dynamic personality. Others to the many Spirit-filled messages he delivered, astounding miracles he performed, and prophesies he saw fulfilled. Still others credit the wartime, oppressive colonial, and general sociopolitical environment of Côte d'Ivoire at the time. But could Harris's deep knowledge of local cultural traditions and his powerful use of primeval myths of creation and its demise have struck a profound chord with his audiences, motivating them to seek change and embrace God's offer of peace? Whatever the ultimate reasons, the result of Harris's lightening journey across the region produced in the view of church historian Adrian Hastings, "the most extraordinary successful one-man evangelical crusade that Africa has ever known."[30]

30. Adrian Hastings, *African Christianity* (New York: Seabury, 1976), 10.

4

The Crucial Role of the Arts in the Identity of Indigenous Peoples in the Southern Philippines

Rocelyn Anog-Madinger

This chapter explores the interplay of an indigenous people's arts with various layers of their identity, especially their cultural-linguistic identity, Christian identity, and personal identity in Christ. As an ongoing study, I continue to engage in community arts workshops and build and maintain relationships with those impacted by these workshops. Participants come mostly from oral cultures. First will be a description of an arts workshop, a community activity where the local arts are studied vis-à-vis the Scriptures. Second will be the stories of how engaging with the arts and Scriptures have impacted some individuals and communities. Finally will be my observations and reflections, concluding with a summary of interviews with the two main personalities quoted in the chapter.

Ethno-Arts is the study of the artistic, creative expressions of an ethnic community that combines the disciplines of ethnomusicology and anthropology. An Ethno-Arts workshop may be as brief as two days or as long as two weeks depending on the needs and availability of participants. The workshops described in this chapter follow the two-track approach introduced by Todd and Mary Saurman.[1] The first track relates to culture, while the second

1. See Mary Beth Saurman and Todd Saurman, "Arts Workshops: Encouraging the Development of Relevant Arts in the Lives of Believers," paper delivered at GCoMM, Bethel University, Saint Paul, MN, 2006.

deals with the Christian Scriptures. For the culture track, participants look at various artistic communication forms within their community including visual arts forms such as local attire, accessories, architecture, colours, designs and patterns, textiles or fabric, bags, etc.; music and song; verbal or oral arts including poetry, stories, riddles, jokes, blessings or curses, greetings, idioms, proverbs or sayings, etc.; and dances, drama, food, and games. We then delve into the context of the art forms asking when and where do they occur? How are they created or performed? Who makes and uses them? Answering these questions enables understanding of the meaning of these forms from the perspective of cultural insiders.

The second track involves a workshop studying passages of Scripture that mention different types of art forms to glean insights. Those passages include 1 Corinthians 14:6–12, to see Paul's thoughts on language and music; Psalm 150, which describes different musical instruments used in praising God; Revelation 7:9–11 which highlights the presence of representatives from every tribe, every tongue, and every nation before God's throne; Psalm 33:1–3 in which the psalmist enjoins the singing of a new song; and Romans 11:33–12:1 which prescribes worship that involves the whole of our lives. Other topics include identity in Christ, worldview, etic-emic (outsider-insider) perspectives, poetic form analysis, contextualization, and cultural redemption. We eventually integrate the two tracks to "look at practical ways to apply what participants discovered for culturally relevant Scripture use, worship, communicating faith to others, community development, literacy, and other community needs."[2]

Participatory approaches and principles of adult learning are used in the sessions. Lectures are intertwined with group dynamics and activities to help students process the content. Some participatory principles and methods include the following: (1) Each voice is valued as important, and workshops are a safe place where participants can be heard and listened to. (2) Local people are recognized as experts with regard to their own culture, expressions, and language. (3) The locals' expertise and experiences are the starting point of the conversations. Finally, (4) we as outsiders and facilitators mostly take the back seat and listen as the participants discover and articulate realizations. These methods allow maximum community participation and dialogue.

Participants are also encouraged to express their insights and synthesize the workshop's lessons in creative and artistic ways. Ideally, the creation of new songs or other relevant art forms is the goal. In such cases, songs or other artistic creations are presented to some representatives of a wider audience to

2. Saurman and Saurman, "Arts Workshops," 3.

gather feedback on clarity, accuracy, and naturalness.[3] Integrative devotions and prayer times are part of the daily schedule as well.

Affirming Identity in the Matigsalug Tribe

Gibs was a twenty-four-year-old man from the Matigsalug tribe, a marginalized indigenous community on the island of Mindanao in southern Philippines. He was sent by his brother, a mother-tongue Bible translator, to attend a two-week "Basic Principles of Ethno-Arts" workshop on his brother's behalf. The workshop participants represented at least twelve language communities and included Bible translators, storying workers, pastors, and cross-cultural workers among others. They spent the first week in a classroom setting where they looked at music and songs, dances, visual arts, poetry, riddles, stories, and other art forms from both their own and other cultures. Then they studied what the Scriptures say, or do not say, about these cultural expressions.

In the second week, all of the participants travelled to Gibs' community to observe a workshop in a community setting. The workshop participants joined members of the Matigsalug community in learning, studying the Scriptures, and worshipping God together with multiple artistic expressions. They witnessed how the elderly Matigsalug constructed and played their musical instruments – like the two-stringed *kuglung* and bamboo zither called *salaroy* – told stories, chanted their songs, wove their mats and baskets, danced their dances, made their accessories, and proudly wore their colourful ethnic attire. The younger Matigsalug observed intently, attempted to dance or play the instruments, and learned to make some uniquely Matigsalug bracelets called *binukol* and leg protectors called *tikos*.

As part of the workshop requirements, Gibs submitted a reflection about his experience. He chose to write a paper and entitled it, "Gibs' Identity." On the top right, he drew an image with only half of their local attire and wrote an explanation across it: "I draw a half pair of my tribal dress. It represents how I see my identity before. I am a Christian, but I am also a *lumad* (native or indigenous) from the Matigsalug tribe. I've been struggling with my identity."

In the Philippines, many times being a member of any minority or indigenous community is not something to celebrate because it is a source of inferiority, shame, and marginalization. When indigenous people attend

3. See Liz Foerster and Mary Saurman, *Overview Workshop for Producing Culturally Relevant Language Development Materials for Mother-Tongue Based Education Program* (Chiangmai: Payap University, 2013).

school, their classmates look at them as different and call them pejorative names, which they endure in silent humiliation. One of Gibs' friends tearfully recounted how outsiders described them as people who live with pigs since the animals live in protected shelters under their houses. The wound surfaced when we asked them to enumerate what makes their culture distinct from others, both positive and negative. Feelings of pride when realizing the wealth of their cultural expressions would be mixed with memories which caused a sense of inferiority.

Gibs confessed that he questioned God: "Why didn't you create me a Cebuano or an Australian instead? Why a Matigsalug!?" Inside the community he saw poverty on many levels. From the outside he felt the demeaning discrimination. Sermons in the church did not help as Matigsalug culture in general was seen as unfit to be integrated into church life. However at the workshop, Gibs realized how much he didn't know about his own culture or how negative his own attitude was toward it. He discovered that his people's cultural expressions were valuable; they were valid and beautiful in God's sight. And if their own art forms had worth, surely they, the Matigsalug, were also precious.

At the end of his reflection paper, Gibs drew a complete picture of his full tribal dress. "I was like the lost son – like I ran away from what my real life is, my tribe. But in this seminar, it's like the Lord let me realize that He's very much interested in the culture of the tribes, because He loves me, He loves our culture." For people like Gibs, their language, musical instruments and songs, dances, and local attire are not simply ornaments, hobbies, trinkets, or pastimes. Though they may be these, they also mean something deeper. The local culture communicates meaningful messages, and it links them to their ancestors and to each other in the community. Their cultural expressions serve as an integral part of the community and connect them with who they are, their heritage, and the intricate web which forms their identity.

At the closing ceremony of the workshop, one of the participants, eighteen-year-old Jenefer who was deeply affected by the week-long event, passionately declared,

> I am Jenefer Mabini, a Matigsalug. I am very thankful for this program that came here. I learned that we can use all things Matigsalug that are not yet used in church. Even if I'm like this – I have curly hair, flat nose, I know that I am a Matigsalug, a tribe chosen by God. The tribes who are praising God will not be complete if the Matigsalug will not be part. I am really grateful that

> even if I am dark, because I am a Matigsalug, I will not be ashamed of it. We learned that we can use our *kuglung* [two-stringed lute] and *salurey* [bamboo zither] in the church; we can use them to praise our God. I am very grateful to be a Matigsalug. I am proud to be a Matigsalug.

Gibs, who was one of the hosts during the ceremony, wore the colourful *tangkulo*, their traditional headdress. I noticed that it looked different from the other headdresses and commented that it was very beautiful. He explained what it meant:

> I am a bit embarrassed to wear this because I just borrowed it. It is usually worn by our elders whose wealth of experience makes them worthy to wear it. But I wear it now as a symbol of my acceptance of what I feel is a call from God: to be a leader of my tribe someday.

Gibs asserted this feeling when he completed his reflection by drawing a whole Matigsalug attire, not just half. He sensed God was reintroducing him to his identity from which he had been running away. God's word spoke at a deeper level when connected to his community's cultural art forms that represented their identity.

In her article "Alliances across Difference," Amber Mayes identifies three levels of human identity: the individual level, the universal human level, and social group level. At the individual level, she says we are different, "we are all completely unique and like no other persons." No thumbmarks or DNA are exactly the same. At the universal level, we are all the same: we all bleed when wounded; we all need air and food and water and people. On the social level, "we are like some people and unlike others. We share experiences, socialization, societal privilege or disadvantage with those in the same social identity group and we differ in our experiences from those in an identity group we don't share."[4] These groups may be according to age, ability, gender, culture, class, race, socioeconomic status, and so on. For most indigenous communities, like that of Gibs, the social group identity most powerfully resonates with them.

However when becoming one with Christ, a new and different identity is given to us. Believers now belong to another social group. Church members historically have often distanced themselves from local cultural expressions

4. Amber Mayes, "Alliances across Difference: Useful strategies for building effective relationships across differences," Organizational Development Network (May 2015), https://intelliven.com/wp-content/uploads/2015/11/Mayes-Amber-Diversity-article.pdf, 2–3.

or practices which were said to have "animistic" associations. This distancing produced some internal tension and often results in the abandonment and loss of cultural identity in order to embrace the new one in Christ. For some, the arts have provided a way to reconcile these two identities.

Finding Identity: The Western Subanon Tribe

On the western side of Mindanao Island, another workshop took place. For decades, the small coastal village of Malayal, Sibuco, Zamboanga del Norte was divided along religious lines. Though the people spoke one common language – Western Subanon – they identified themselves as either Alliance (evangelical), Roman Catholic, or Tanud Palin, the local religion. They could not bring themselves to be together under one roof, especially if that roof was owned by one of the other groups. Many lived suspicious of the worship and faith practices of the others.

Then came an event that broke through the fears and division – an Ethno-Arts workshop that aimed to document Subanon music and dance forms. Sharon, a mother-tongue translator of the Subanon Bible, had always dreamed of this. Her vision was to document their rich art forms that were at risk of being soon lost if nothing was done to preserve them. The young people of their church did not know much about their own culture, but Sharon felt that their music and dance, though long used to worship and appease spirits, needed to be brought back to worship the one true God. She wanted her fellow believers to discover, understand, and value what they had as Subanon people, and she believed they could simultaneously be Christians and Subanon.

Together with others who shared this vision, Sharon organized an Ethno-Arts workshop that included a visit to the local religion's worship house. This was the only place she knew where the Subanon instruments were still played and the dances danced. After she fasted and prayed for wisdom and favour, the Tanud Palin agreed to have their music and dance documented and said that the workshop participants would be welcome to enter their building and witness their music, song, and dance.

On the first day of the workshop, all of the participants from both the evangelical and Roman Catholic churches trekked to the worship house of the Tanud Palin. For the first few minutes, everyone could sense tension and uncertainty in the air. The Tanud Palin, even though the place was theirs, also did not seem at ease with the crowd. After prayer, the music began – an elderly woman struck the opening notes of the *kulintangan*, small, horizontally laid and embossed gongs, and was immediately followed on cue by the playing of three large hanging gongs, *og gagung*. The men began dancing to the music, solemnly moving around the circle they created to be followed by the women who took their places and danced in the same manner, but with a slower tempo.

Little by little, the audience warmed to what was going on. A dance "contest" followed as the *kulintangan* played a more spirited beat and the leader stirred the audience who sat around to give shouts or hoots of affirmation as they saw fit to spur the dancers on. After lunch, the elders were ready to teach, and the audience was called to participate. In the middle of the afternoon, children who were off from school began curiously peeking in, and they were all ushered inside. The smaller children then unabashedly joined the dancing, eliciting loud applause from their elders. The participants who earlier had sober faces now donned relaxed smiles. The bigger crowd, the livelier music, and the more joyful dancing all added to a festive atmosphere and a lightening of the once tense mood.

When it was time to end, leaders and representatives of the groups gave short speeches. All of them expressed gratitude, and not a few had tears in their eyes. Those who spoke were visibly moved, attempting to control their emotions. They all said this was the first time all three groups had gathered together in one place, and for a brief moment, forgot their religious differences. The community overcame their fear and were one, and together in unity they celebrated with their very own music and dance their Subanon identity.

Through their own music and dance, a divided community reminded themselves that they shared one cultural and linguistic identity. Yes, they spoke the same language, but now they celebrated with the same sounds, colour, and movements that shouted they were one. They indeed belonged to each other in a way that transcended their differing religious beliefs. The Western Subanon believers, just like Gibs, realized how much they did not know about their own culture, and how ignorant they were. After the workshop, one church worker testified that she was very happy because she previously did not know what it meant to be a Subanon. Sharon's intended message that the church members need not leave their cultural identity behind to be Christians was clearly conveyed. For many years, they had sung mostly Western Christian praise and worship songs and played Western instruments like guitars, drums, and keyboards. Then as they explored their own cultural expressions, they realized from the Scriptures that they had the freedom to worship using their own language, dances, musical styles, and instruments. Indeed, they could be Subanon and Christian at the same time. Their expressions were even more appropriate than the Western forms they had rigidly adopted as "Christian." They were free. Free to be themselves as God created and viewed them.

Concluding Observations

First, Christians from indigenous communities often struggle to accept, or are detached from, their cultural identity. Their sense of identity is not only at the personal or individual level, but even more at the communal or social level.

Second, the message of the gospel speaks strongly as it addresses the social level identity. The message of our identity in Christ is better understood when it celebrates our unique cultural identity as well. Giving space and time to rediscover a community's local art forms serves as a platform on which members of different generations can come together. The younger learn from and listen to the older, and the older feel honoured and valued by the younger. This interaction also helps in strengthening identity as the younger ones connect with their roots. The Bible shows how different art forms like song, dance, riddle, poetry, storytelling, and visual arts are used for worship, communication, and expression and lead to a sense of freedom in using unique creative cultural expressions.

Third, affirming indigenous cultural art forms and encouraging their use serves as a bridge to an appreciation or acceptance of cultural-linguistic identity, and a deeper appreciation of God's love for them as a people. The message of God's love becomes more meaningful when connected with and expressed through the communication forms that resonate with the recipients. *Finally,* Cultural art forms are tools or communicative channels that local believers should explore for reaching out and being a blessing to non-believers in their community.

Postscript

Gibs, whose story is told in this chapter, has since witnessed some of the elderly members of his tribe come to church because they heard the traditional instruments being played. With his cousin who participated in the workshop, Gibs now shares his story with other minority communities through Ethno-Arts events or camps. He knows that he is not the only one ashamed to be a member of an indigenous tribe, and he reminds people that all cultures are created equal – all have their uniqueness and flaws. He exhorts them that change can happen by embracing who they are, not by running away from their identity or pretending they are something else. He has seen strong emotional responses from some of his audiences as he concludes his sharing with a prayer of repentance, asking them to repent from looking down on themselves and for questioning God for creating them the way he did.

Sharon now testifies that previously her people had been taught not to use their own music, song, and dance because it was demonic and had been used to worship other deities. But now they have experienced the freedom to use their cultural forms in the worship of the one true God. They have since started to create new songs in the Subanon language for their Sunday worship and other gatherings accompanied with their traditional instruments and dances. The church sees the importance of their cultural arts as being part of their Subanon identity. Sharon, a linguist, commends the work of Ethno-Arts as part of "language and culture revitalization, maintaining diversity in this God-created world."

Since this chapter has drawn on experiences among indigenous peoples in the Philippines, we include below the legal definition of such groups as contained in the Philippine Republic Act 8371:

> *Philippine Republic Act No. 8371*
>
> Indigenous Cultural Communities (ICC) or Indigenous Peoples (IP) refer to a group of people or homogenous societies identified by self-ascription and ascription by others, who have continuously lived as organized community on communally bounded and defined territory, and who have, under claims of ownership since time immemorial, occupied, possessed and utilized such territories, sharing common bonds of language, customs, traditions and other distinctive cultural traits, or who have, through resistance to political, social and cultural inroads of colonization, non-indigenous religions and cultures, became historically differentiated from the majority of Filipinos.[5]

I wish to acknowledge the help of Ricky Emboc and Sharon Bulalang in personal interviews and the insights gained from the following sources: Paul Hiebert, *Anthropological Insights for Missionaries* (Grand Rapids, MI: Baker Books, 1985); James R. Krabill, ed., *Worship and Mission for the Global Church* (Pasadena, CA: William Carey Library, 2013); Brian Schrag and Kathleen van Buren, *Make Arts for a Better Life: A Guide for Working With Communities* (New York: Oxford University Press, 2018); and Thomas Tufte and Paulo Metaloupos, *Participatory Communication: A Practical Guide* (Washington, DC: World Bank, 2009).

5. Philippine Republic Act 8371, https://www.officialgazette.gov.ph/1997/10/29/republic-act-no-8371/

Part Two

Primal Traditions and Christianity in Northeast India

5

Toward a Kuki Contextual Theology of *Khankho*

Jangkholam Haokip

Writing an indigenous theology is like building a house with no ready-made tools. Here you are put in a situation that demands self-determination, courage to imagine and develop tools, and finally to do the construction in such a way that all will find it a good house. The main challenge is not the theology as such but the courage to embrace the indigenous people's life questions as a valid theological context for the articulation of faith. It is to overcome the fear of making "mistakes," or even committing "heresy" in expressing who Christ is in the indigenous context. This chapter takes the risk of discerning the footprints of God among indigenous people, believing that even "heresies" can make sense to people if made in the quest for a relevant Christ. This chapter argues that the God-given values in indigenous people's cultures are capable of reflecting their creator and his plan for salvation.

A Glimpse of the Context

A church elder, who was a member of the governing board of the integral missional project I had the privilege to help, developed a mysterious condition that resulted in the end to his life. Every day at dawn, he went to church to pray. On a particular morning in 2009, he noticed a sign, a *Doi* or omen, planted at night at his house gate. Being a committed and radical faith-practising Christian, the elder started to dig out the elements of the omen saying that the God whom he worships is stronger than all evil powers, and no omen would do any harm to him. As he dug deeper, he discovered stuff like a betel nut, a paan leaf, a bird's nest, and lastly an egg, which he unfortunately broke. In traditional belief, the preservation of the egg would have rendered the omen powerless. But its destruction exposed him to the evil power, and within a few days of the incident his belly swelled and continued to grow for the next few weeks until he could breathe no more and died. The traditional belief is that he would not have died had the egg not been broken since the power of the omen would not have been released. Despite the challenges of this situation, the elder refused to consult local diviners and chose to put his trust in God, thus dying a faithful Christian death.

This incident raises many questions. We believe that God, the all-knowing and all-powerful One, can do anything he wishes for the sake of his people. But this kind of experience reveals the absence of theological reflection and pastoral response to the reality of the spirit world. In other words, concerns about spirits and spiritual warfare have not been given adequate emphasis in our inherited Christianity despite the huge need of indigenous people for help in precisely this area. This is despite the fact that the gospel was presented as teaching that Christ has overpowered Satan, and hence those who believe should have no fear of evil spirits. Indeed, most tribal people turn to Christianity to escape the constant fear of evil powers. Yet the absence of theological reflection and pastoral practice responding to such situations is a sign of the denial of the tribal people and their existential issues for theological articulation and expression. In a sense, indigenous people are outside of the theological vision within which the kingdom of God is understood and said to be realised.

This exclusion of indigenous people's issues in theological reflection is at the same time the exclusion of their methodological concerns. How do we deal with the reality of spirits and the spirit world around us methodologically? The scientific world and its methodology, while of importance and great value, is inadequate to address this concern. Theological seminaries and academic studies do not prepare students to deal with this issue because the presence of spiritual powers cannot be tested and verified scientifically. Working with indigenous people, therefore, needs an additional theological perspective and methodology.

The Methodology

Unlike traditional systematic theology, in the context we are concerned with here, theological methodology and the actual creation of theology need to merge together in a closer dialogue with each other. Ideally, methodology precedes theology, but a theology and theological vision derived from a given context has to influence its methodology. The Vietnamese-born, American Catholic theologian Peter C. Phan beautifully argues for this approach in his visionary article, "Method in Liberation Theologies."[1] Phan draws upon biblical insights to support his view by quoting the metaphor of putting "new wine into new wineskins" (Matt 9:17). This metaphor suggests that every new situation needs a new methodology, and ideally speaking, one should not apply a methodology developed elsewhere for a new situation. Old methodologies are developed to deal with particular historical and cultural situations. Phan observes that flexibility of methodologies is exactly what he sees happening in liberation theologies, and for that very reason they will continue to survive in the future in spite of many criticisms.[2]

Another pioneering Asian theologian, Kosuke Koyama, discussing the question of whether methodology should precede theology, responds by asking: "How can they know where they are going before they start walking?"[3] In the context of Asia in general, and of indigenous people in particular, methodologies developed in the narrow approach of the Western worldview are inadequate to deal with the wide-ranging and complex issues of the lived realities of indigenous people. Hence it is undesirable to approach such contexts with predetermined answers to urgent existential questions. A theological journey in the context of indigenous peoples cannot be preprogrammed, and we must be ready to encounter many surprises on an untrodden path.

It was for this reason that Koyama chose to try and "see the face of God in the faces of the people" instead of following received methodologies developed to address his own different context. Koyama suggested that it is not a matter of devising a different application of a received theological method, but that the inherited method may itself be inappropriate in different cultural settings, including the indigenous context. For this reason, Koyama moved away from the traditional understanding of methodology and exhibited creativity in his *Water Buffalo Theology* to demonstrate how methodologies can be developed in the light of given contexts, and risked his own marginalisation in the world of academic theology by putting into practice his deep convictions.

1. Peter C. Phan, "Method in Liberation Theologies," *Theological Studies* 61 (2000): 40–63.

2. Phan, "Method in Liberation Theologies," 63.

3. Kosuke Koyama, *Water Buffalo Theology* (Maryknoll, NY: Orbis, 1999), x. See also Kosuke Koyama, *No Handle on the Cross: An Asian Meditation on the Crucified Mind* (London: SCM, 1976). Another example of theology arising from a specific Asian context is Kazoh Kitamori, *Theology of the Pain of God* (London: SCM, 1966), originally published in 1946 in response to the nuclear devastation of the cities of Hiroshima and Nagasaki.

Approaching the Challenge of Contextual Tribal Theology

We need a similar approach to the sacred task of discerning and tracing the footprints of God among indigenous peoples. Far from depending on ready-made tools, our attempt is to discern and reclaim kingdom values in the history of the people, which means revisiting their myths, folklores, and oral traditions – the rich resources we have mistakenly discarded. We need to go back to the dustbins and see if we have thrown away something made of gold. Putting this in the form of questions asked by the Kuki people of the mountainous region of Manipur in Northeast India –

- Who brought our ancestors out of the *Khul* (cave) and sustained them until the arrival of the first missionary?
- Where did the concept and tradition of *Khankho* come from?
- Who gave the Kukis the idea that our security is in the hands of others, and therefore we must live peacefully with others including with nature and the spirits? Is there any other source of good things apart from God?

Traditional Kuki life was grounded in, sustained, and directed by the vision of *Khankho*. Life was viewed as interdependent, relational, and inclusive, and was shared in a community expressed through integrity, honesty, love, justice, fairness, and selfless service of one another. There were evils in the society but no capital punishment was allowed in dealing with them. Life was considered sacred; hence no human could take the life of another human being. Our forefathers believed in the existence of one God but worshipped him differently in each household without any doctrinal conflict. It is high time to ask, if *Khankho* sustained the people for many generations, providing them with indigenous wisdom and skills to relate with one another in a community and to exist in harmony with the natural world in an even wider community, how could *Khankho* have been dismissed as "evil"? If all good things come from only one source, God, how can we say that God was totally absent from the Kukis before the coming of the first missionary? We shall explore certain aspects of *Khankho* and suggest what might be viewed as signs of God's act of salvation among the people.

Concept of God

Before we attempt to discern what might be considered part of God's wider plan for salvation among indigenous people, it is important to discuss their concept of God and how that view might enrich our contemporary understanding of the Supreme Being. As indicated above, traditional Kuki people believed in one God but worshipped him differently in each household without any doctrinal conflict. Their belief in a monotheistic God was reflected in their rituals and ceremonies. At the *Hun* ceremony at the end of every year, for instance, the whole village gathered and organized a thanksgiving offering to one God, praying for new blessings on the entire village for the new year. At every *Hun* ceremony, the village priest would make ten *mithuns* and ten gongs from clay and offer them to God at the altar called *Khomol*.

Apart from such community rituals, each eligible household kept *Doibom*, a religious symbol of God's presence and a focus for the worship of God through it when and as required. In other words, God was accessible to all, and the people formed their own understanding of God without any spirit of competition or superiority. They did not have room for a religious superiority complex in their theological framework, and such conflict was inconsistent with the *Khankho* way of life! In fact, while they remained firm in their belief in a monotheistic God, they did not have a definitive term and expression for God. Like the use of silence in the Hebrew tradition of YHWH, for instance, they addressed God as *Pu Hou-Pa Hou* (that which our forebears worshipped) to avoid the danger of making a mistake in trying to be specific about God. They also called God *Pathennu-Pathenpa* (Mother God-Father God) to capture the reality of God as the one who cares for us both as a father and a mother. These are not the signs of a polytheistic religion but rather a recognition of the inadequacy of human knowledge to explain the indescribable reality of God.[4]

A truly indigenous and biblical theology is firmly rooted in a monotheistic faith, but is expressed humbly before God (Mic 6:8). Indigenous people knew the limits of human capacity to know God and recognised that some aspects of knowledge belonged to the realm of God alone. Their understanding of God was monotheistic, non-judgemental, and communitarian.

The tradition of *An-Lo-Tol*, a "passing of a basket of food to others" in the family worship of God provides a fuller view of indigenous practice. Here all the members of a household sit together in a circle at *Sutphung* (the middle

4. Writing about the Herero people in East Africa, Theo Sundermeier describes a conversation with one of his African students during a car journey in which he asked the student about the meaning of the traditional name for God: *Njambi*. The student became very uneasy in this conversation, and when asked what the problem was, he replied, "I grew up with my pious grandmother and was brought up in the Christian faith. However, this name for God was so holy for us that we could never use it. If we did, we were heavily punished. And I find myself sitting next to a white man, and he uses this old Herero name for God as if it were of no significance!" Theo Sundermeier, *The Individual and Community in African Traditional Religion* (Hamburg: Lit Verlag, 1998), 160.

and most important pillar of the house) and pass a small basket of food to each other. It is passed several times among the family members with words of prayer, and finally the head of the household concludes the worship. Thus, all family members including men, women, and children have a role in the worship of God. Kuki spiritual practice was inclusive and embraced the whole family in a participatory worship service.

An Understanding of *Khankho*

Good academic writing does not usually begin with a negative sentence, but an indigenous theology does because of the inadequacy of available terms as well as the richness of indigenous knowledge. I have been struggling to define *Khankho* for many years, but still find myself unable to do it satisfactorily. While some aspects of indigenous knowledge are difficult to define in the English language, others are hard to explain in the form of writing. This difficulty does not mean that we should give up our attempts but rather explore alternative ways and means to understand the tradition.

The term *Khankho* is made up of two different words, *khan* and *kho*. *Khan* means "to grow," "to develop," but here it means "to behave" or to lead a life in tune with the deepest values of the culture. Similarly, the term *kho* in general means "village," but here it means "sensibility," or awareness of the needs of one's surroundings and the conduct of life in response to it. In short, *Khankho* is *leading a life in tune with the culture grounded in love, care, fairness, and justice. It expresses connectedness, interdependence, and sharing in the celebration of life in community.*

Given the definition of those words, those who live *Khankho* well are called *Khankho he* (someone who knows/lives out *Khankho*), and those who do not are called *Khankho helou* (those who do not know/practice *Khankho*). For instance, someone who does not care about others, or who fails to perform his or her duty as *tucha* or *becha* (customary duties toward others) are called *Khankho helou.* But here again, "knowing" is not merely an intellectual knowledge, nor is it simply performing customary duties toward others but involves the sharing of life together with others in a community. In contrast, *Khankho helou* is considered the opposite; the "*kho*" in *Khankho* also means "sense," as in senseless, meaningless, or lifeless. In this case, from the perspective of the Kuki worldview, a *Khankho helou* is like someone who is lifeless, without a sense of even pain or happiness, and so is not really a person!

The opposite to *Khankho helou* is *Khankho he.* As mentioned above, words are not enough to explain this concept and its outworking in practice. Cognitive understanding alone cannot capture the vision of *Khankho*! Sometimes attempts are made to define the concept using various arts, and at the Bethesda Khankho Institute in Manipur, artwork is displayed on the roadsides so that people can understand part of the meaning of *Khankho* through a visual image. An annual event is organized to live out the values of *Khankho* in the community by supporting vulnerable people.

Traditionally, the widely used story told to illustrate *Khankho* is that of Lendou and his brother.[5] Early in their childhood, Lendou and his brother lost their father, but to add to their tragedy, their mother eloped with a man while they were still very young. Having realised that their mother was missing, Lendou and his brother ran after her and her lover in order to get their mother back. They crossed several mountains and valleys until they reached an uncrossable river, at which point they turned back disappointed, tired, and hungry. On their way home they found a tiny Job's tear seed which they shared equally between them. This is a bedtime story of *Khankho* passed down through the generations that, along with other such stories, shapes the lives of the people by encouraging truthfulness, integrity, creation care, and so on.

The closest concept to *Khankho* in the Bible is the vision of "shalom," the promised kingdom of love, peace, justice, fairness, well-being, tranquillity, prosperity, and security. Shalom is the manifestation of divine grace, the foretaste of the future kingdom of God here on earth. *Khankho* was and remains the foundation, the binding code, the guide and at the same time the vision of traditional Kuki community developed under the knowledge of God. It emerges from the land to meet the needs of the people and their environment as part of God's plan for salvation. With this conviction about the indigenous tradition of *Khankho*, we shall now attempt to identify and trace the footprints of God among the people.

Walk Carefully Lest You Disturb Peace with the Unseen Beings

In a theology of *Khankho*, reality is not limited to what can be known through our five senses. Indigenous people believe that there is another world, or a spirit world that can be related to through dreams and visions. They believe that although spirits cannot be seen, they are real and active in the world. Because of this belief the question of fairness, justice, and cordial relationships with all in an indigenous community is important, since violation of ethical obligations within the community can result in sanctions originating from the spiritual

5. See Lal Dena, *Hmar Folk Tales* (Delhi: Scholar, 1995).

realm. When walking through the jungle, children are firmly instructed by their parents not to walk carelessly so that they do not disturb the peace with the unprovoked, unseen beings. Indigenous people also believe in malevolent spirits, and this reality plays a significant role in encouraging people to lead a life of integrity.

Conversion to Christianity brought about changes, including the removal of the fear of evil spirits among the converts by proclaiming Jesus as the conqueror over all spiritual powers. But sadly, many Christians seem to have taken only the name of Jesus and left behind his message, the call to a life of discipleship which has much in common with *Khankho,* including leading a life of integrity, fairness, and the other features mentioned above. By claiming to be born-again Christians, too many converts appear to think that the rest of kingdom concerns are taken care of, and they are free to do anything in any way they choose. The end result is seen in the increasing gap between the rich and the poor, the ecological crisis, the general decline of morality, and the problem of evil spirits and their revived influence within the society.

Here then the theological task is about claiming and strengthening the message of the gospel, reflected in and anticipated by *Khankho*, for the healing of the world through Christ. In meeting Christ, we do not abandon our cultures but see them being perfected in him. All the transformative elements of *Khankho* find their identity and meaning in Christ. The salvific work of Christ on earth is seen in the way that Jesus resisted and overcame the temptation of Satan to worship the gods of materialism, hedonism, and egoism (Luke 4:1–13). Finally, on the cross for eternal salvation, Jesus gave himself up for others. In doing indigenous Christian theology, we do not simply take the name of Jesus and pronounce it to evil spirits as if we are wonder workers but rather strive together to lead a life of integrity in our real-life situations in the light of the Christ events.[6] Theology concerns and strengthens the continuous walk of faith in humility in the path of God's integral salvation.

Khankho and Creation Care

Not only do indigenous people take the spiritual world seriously, they also treat what has been called the *natural world, the rest of creation,* with respect and even with awe. Creation is a living world infused with spirit and so capable of knowing joy, pain, distress, and hope. For this reason, the natural world

6. See Paul Lelen Haokip, *Relevance of Thempu in Pastoral Ministry: A Socio-Theological Perspective* (New Delhi: BKI/CWI, 2020).

is treated with respect and care. For example, a cultivator of rice regards the plants as living things requiring care, so that even bad words may not be spoken against them. We may ask whether this perception of nature as what might be called a sacrament is closer to a biblical understanding of the created world than the modern approach which shows no respect for the earth, for animals and plants, but treats them as objects to be exploited for pleasure or for profit. Which of these views is closest to Pauline theology regarding nature wherein the natural world is said to feel pain and to share the hope of liberation (Rom 8:18–25)?

Unlike the traditional Christian teaching filtered through European culture, the indigenous concept of sin is breaking relationships with others, including nature. This concept is clear in the *Tol-Theh* ritual performance involving the clearing of ground (*Tol* - ground, *theh* – clearing), a ceremony performed in order to remove sin from the land.[7] The belief is that when a person commits sin, or breaks a relationship by hurting someone, the earth suffers infertility, and the remedy requires the guilty person to perform a ceremony of cleansing the ground from that sin. This clearing of the ground is done by visualizing the way in which a pig clears up the ground. Human sin thus has both horizontal and vertical effects, so the remedy must include both healing the human relationship and restoration of the fertility of the ground. A similar picture is found in Genesis 4:12 where God says to Cain that the earth would no longer yield fruit for him because he had killed his brother, Abel. Reading this text from an indigenous perspective can help us to understand that human sin affects nature and that understanding, in turn, encourages us to care for our world. Another parallel is found in the book of Job where the issue of land and justice are inseparably connected (Job 31:38–40).

In such a context, the worldview of indigenous people of Northeast India is similar to that of people who believe in traditional religions in Africa, as can be seen from James Kraybill's chapter in this book. So the frequently cited African term *Ubuntu,* "I am because we are," is close to the indigenous Kuki understanding of life as consisting of a web of relationships in which one cannot exist without others. The phrase "*Khat louva khat phatheilou*" means "you cannot do without others," and in an indigenous community, everyone is related to everyone else, and un-relatedness is an unthinkable condition. It is against *Khankho*. On the basis of and for the sake of *Khankho,* villages were established with the head of a clan made a chief who is responsible to

7. See Tarun Goswami, *Kuki Life and Lore* (Halflong: North Cachar Hill District Council, 1985).

discharge his responsibilities selflessly for the well-being of his villagers, and vice versa. These relationships include those outside the community through a specific social institution. For example a person is related to his mother's side as *tucha* with certain responsibilities to be performed, while in a similar way, he is related to all the members of the society through the institution of various relationship systems and duties. To those outside of the community, a person can relate to others through the institution of *Jol* (friend) which often binds people in a manner that is even stronger than blood relationships. In this manner, life and duties in a community are inspired and guided by the God-given *Khankho*.

The idea of interdependence is clearly expressed in the way success is understood in indigenous cultures as an achievement of something in agreement with and in support of others, including the natural world. Success is not about an individual person striving hard alone and achieving something as an isolated, single being, but rather it is in establishing and maintaining cordial relationships with others that success is possible. This perspective is clear in *Sa-Ai* and *Chang-Ai*. *Sa-Ai* is a celebration of hunted animals which includes the belief that at the point of a person's death, that person will be safely escorted to heaven by their hunted wild animal, which could be a tiger. Similarly, a woman will be safely escorted to heaven when she dies by the fruit of her successful cultivation of rice. In both cases, success never happens without first establishing cordial relationships with and support of the spirits of nature. To obtain this relationship, both men and women have to seek to establish good relationships with animals (for men) and rice (for women) by performing certain rituals, such as *Salha-Kou/Changlha-Kou* or the ceremony of invoking spirits of animals or rice, and behaving carefully with nature. Here, concepts like success or development can never be the achievement of an isolated individual but are understood horizontally in the sense that true success is only possible if everyone, including nature, rejoices with you. If in the modern world of global capitalism the worth of people is judged by how much money they make in the shortest possible time, the worth of people in the indigenous tradition is determined by how their "success" contributes to the well-being of many people and to the sustaining and flourishing of the natural world. "Success" is inseparable from establishing cordial relationships.

Khankho and Indigenous Spirituality

The incantation of *Ganlhaina* accompanying animal sacrifice indicates the God-human-nature relationships in the indigenous worldview. The priest who performs the ritual, the animal to be sacrificed, and God to whom the prayer is being made are all participants in the prayer. The priest prays in dialogue and agreement with God and nature. The incantation of *Ganlhaina* includes these words:

> O you cock! You are the progeny of my white and black hens. Today, I am not doing this (here the priest means the action of cutting the cock) for the sake of your meat. I am not doing this like those who strike the palm trees with their axes just to try how sharp their axes are; or like the others who cut the branches of the Banian tree wantonly. I am performing this job today, so that you may call the spirits of the paddy and the spirits of mim seeds, and as such, may you not be sad or be regretful.[8]

Having justified his intention to sacrifice to the cock, the priest then seeks God's instruction for the actual killing of the bird. He holds the cock by its head, and another person grasps its body. The priest then puts the blunt side of a sickle, or *dao*, on the stretched neck of the cock and chants the following:

> O god of heaven! Would it be proper for me to do like this. (Here the priest means cutting the cock's neck by the blunt side of the sickle.) The God of heaven answers (through the mouth of the priest): O man, do not do like that; but cut the cock's neck with the sharp edge of the sickle. If you do like this you would be happy and healthy in body and mind, and you will be successful in everything that you may do.[9]

Our interest in this ritual is not to reintroduce the practice of sacrifice but to observe the theology reflected in the ritual or prayer. The incantation shows that the priest acted not on his own wish but in dialogue and agreement with nature and with God. The priest does not carry out the killing of the chicken on his own but seeks God's guidance and justification (*kikaona*) lest he hurt the spirit of the sacrificial animal. In other words, the priest does not regard nature as merely a ritual instrument, or a thing, but as a subject that needs fair treatment, respect, and justice. A similar idea is seen in Exodus 23:5 where the Lord says, "If you see the donkey of someone who hates you fallen down under its load, do not leave it there; be sure you help them with it." What is

8. Goswami, *Kuki Life and Lore*: 161–162.

9. Goswami, 162.

clear is that the animal, no matter who owns it or for what purpose it is being used, must be treated with justice and fairness.

Another important point here is the agreement between the priest, the sacrificial cock, and *Pathen* (God) and their wholehearted involvement in the ritual so that the act is not merely that of the individual priest but one in which the cock and *Pathen* are also involved. Sacrifice is a communal affair involving not only humans but also nature and God the creator to whom prayers are made. In this, God in his love and compassion is involved in the act and the process of prayer. In other words, God himself guides our intercession so that we care not only for ourselves but also for nature.

We have said that excluding the reality of the spirit world in theologizing in tribal areas involves neglecting a crucial component of the traditional worldview. At the same time, we must acknowledge that a renewed emphasis on spirits can be destructive unless it is done carefully. In Kuki mythical tradition it was said that human beings at one time could see and eliminate spirits. Fearing extinction, the spirits appealed to God who in response instructed them to put *chollaivon* (zest with a black centre) at the source of human drinking water. When this was done and humans drank the water, black spots appeared in their eyes and prevented them from seeing the spirits. As a result, the old conflict with the spirit world resumed. The consciousness of spirits stems from this tradition and led many Kuki to embrace Christianity believing that Christ is the Victor over all spiritual powers. Today care is needed to ensure that a renewed emphasis upon spirit power and the contextualization of the Christian faith do not end up causing people to believe that Christian faith involves an uncritical return to the pre-Christian worldview. Instead, theology in such a context must equip the church to discern and reinterpret the spiritual power and effectively express the authority of Christ over all the powers of the world.

Paul Hiebert, a well-known missionary anthropologist, observed that the problem of dualism led Western societies, including some Christians, to deny the reality of spirits except in heaven, and hence caused people to believe they could remove the need for spiritual warfare. Their focal point became the evil within social and political systems, and the church understood their role as fighting against poverty, injustice, and oppression. While there is clear biblical justification for such an approach, eliminating the spiritual dimension left indigenous peoples without biblical responses to their fear of spiritual powers. Hiebert recognised the crucial importance of this dimension for traditional societies and urged its recovery as crucial for the good news of millions of people in the majority world.[10]

This issue brings us back to the tragic story of the elder with which this chapter began. He believed the omen to be deadly but determined to face its power believing that subordinate spirits could not harm him, and he continued to emphasize even on his death bed that the omen could not harm him. The questions which arise are these: do spirits have power over the lives of believers? What is the role of faith in Christ before the power of spirits? How do we support those who suffer attacks, and in what manner do we develop an indigenous theology of spiritual warfare?

A Call to Mission

Behind the tradition of *Khankho* is a worldview in which reality is seen as a web of relationships and life is seen as interdependent. One cannot live without others, and the survival and security of each person depends upon others. When life is seen as interdependent, people have a sense of respect and see the necessity for peaceful coexistence among human beings and between humans and nature. Indigenous people have lived close to nature for centuries and as a result have gained knowledge and wisdom concerning that world. They have become local experts in relating to and taking care of nature. Increasingly, Western scholars are recognising the unique and distinctive knowledge of traditional peoples, and even within modern biotechnology industries is growing interest in what these scholars now call "indigenous knowledge." Stephen Ellis and Gerrie ter Haar comment that the knowledge of plants and herbs possessed by tribal peoples across the earth is "a potential boon to the whole of humanity." However, they go on to point out that when such indigenous knowledge is discovered by Western scientists to be "scientifically exact and commercially useful," resulting in the production of patented drugs, "it ceases to be considered as indigenous knowledge and is reclassified as scientific knowledge."[11]

---

10. See Paul Hiebert "Spiritual Warfare and Worldviews," at http://globalmissiology.org/index.php/paul-g-hiebert-legacy. PDF Accessed 25/02/2022. See also Paul Hiebert, *Transforming Worldviews: An Anthropological Understanding of How People Change* (Grand Rapids: Baker Academic, 2008). Especially chapter 5, 'Worldviews of Small-Scale Oral Societies': 105–122.

11. Stephen Ellis and Gerrie ter Haar, *Worlds of Power: Religious Thought and Political Practice in Africa* (London: Hurst, 2004), 194. They conclude that "the world is engaged in a massively important debate about what types of knowledge are appropriate and applicable for whom," 195.

Despite such recognition and like nature itself, tribal peoples are victims of aggressive economic policies and practices in the name of development. Indeed they are victims of what is called progress! Despite their rich resources and experiences, indigenous people and their cultural values have not yet been incorporated into the global search for ecological peace, and neither has their theological wisdom been recognised and incorporated within the understanding of the gospel and the mission of God in world Christianity. As David Smith's chapter in this book demonstrates, however, change is occurring, and the "voices from the margins" are increasingly being recognised as having a critical contribution to make to the witness of the one Body of Christ on earth. Therefore, we must incorporate indigenous knowledge, for instance the concept of sin and its remedy, into our search for a theological response to the quest for climate justice. This is the time to return to the indigenous communities and take them along with us on the journey together to care for nature. Incorporating indigenous cultural resources will help us immensely in caring for creation as part of our commitment to Christ and his mission.

This reflection has taken risks in an attempt to discern and express what could be considered the footprints of God and God's act of salvation among indigenous people. A special focus is given to *Khankho*, and the meaning of the gospel of Christ was explored through the lens of that culture. Attempts are made to articulate and express the salvific work of Christ in light of *Khankho*, knowing that even "heresies" made in a genuine search for truth can make sense if God blesses them. Knowledge and wisdom, including theological knowledge, emerge from the land, and this is the contribution which can be offered to the human family from this place.

6

The Quest for Meaning in Boro Orality

Songram Basumatary

The Boro people of Assam, also known as Bodo, are one of the largest indigenous tribes of Northeast India. They are believed to be the descendants of the Mongoloid race and created the first culture and civilization in the Brahmaputra valley as aborigines with kingdoms and kings of their own.[1] The population is concentrated on the northern bank of the great Brahmaputra River, beginning at the Dhuburi and Kokrajhar districts in the extreme west, to the Lakhimpur and Dhemaji districts in the east. The Boros are also found in small numbers in the states of Meghalaya, Tripura, Nagaland, and West Bengal, as well as in the neighbouring countries of Nepal and Bangladesh. Altogether the population is over three million, most of whom follow the Boro indigenous religion, *Bathou Dhwrwm,* or *Brahma Dhwrwm*, a cognate religion related to Hinduism. There are also significant numbers of Boro Christians.

1. The terms described here are used ambiguously in ways that can be confusing for strangers. Nineteenth-century colonial orthography established "Bodo" as the generic name denoting a broad linguistic family belonging to Tibeto-Burman subfamily of the Tibeto-Chinese family of languages. The term "Boro" denotes a particular homogenous tribe within the Bodo family who speak one common language. Therefore, the term "Boro" is consciously used in this chapter. "Kachari" is also a generic term for a number of groups speaking a more or less common language and claiming common racial ancestry. For detailed discussion, see Thomas Pulloppillil and Jacob Aluckal, eds., *The Bodos: Children of Bhullumbutter* (Guwahati, Delhi: Spectrum, 1997); Edward Gait, *A History of Assam* (Guwahatti: LBS, 1983 [1926]), 236; Sidney Endle, *The Kacharis* (Delhi: Low Price, 1990 [1910]), xvi, 3–4; Monirul Hussain, "Tribal Question in Assam," *Economic and Political Weekly* 27, no. 20–21 (May 1992): 1047; and Kanaklal Barua, *Studies in the Early History of Assam,* ed. M. Neog (Gauhati/Jorhat: Assam Sahitya Sabha, 1973), 207–20.

The Boro community is rich in beliefs and values-filled socioreligious customs and traditions engraved in orality, the storehouse of their worldview, philosophy, and entire lifeworld. Therefore, although the authenticity of orality is doubted and its value discredited by so-called enlightened minds, the authority of oral tradition among the Boro community remains significant. The extent of the use of oral customs, practices, and values suggests that orality remains the sacred text for this people with authority over their socioreligious and cultural life. As most of the contents of orality are "belief narratives," it governs the life of the people and community as a whole.[2]

However, we can see a gradual shift from orality to textuality over the course of time, and Boro scholars debate this trend. Some hold the view that the preservation of oral traditions through textualizing is an unavoidable necessity for the future of Boro identity. In the face of the threat of assimilation to dominant cultures and fear of extinction due to modernism, preserving these traditions is sometimes seen as impossible. Therefore, Boro intellectuals began to recognise the need to document "folk narratives" for their preservation, not merely as historical records but also as continuing foundations for Boro identity. In contrast is a strong view that the oral traditions should be maintained in their original forms through performance and so passed on to future generations to maintain the unique character of Boro society.

Whatever the view may be, scholars are making renewed efforts to study Boro orality as one of the components of study in Bodo literature departments at the university level. Analysis of oral traditions around the world has revitalized the quest for meanings in orality, and attempts are being made to study Boro oral traditions for ontological and epistemological meanings. Keeping such challenges and prospects in mind, I present in this chapter some of the most important contents of Boro orality and analyse them to find meanings that may provide a certain impetus for peaceful coexistence and harmonious community living.

Orality: Concepts and Methods

The dictionary definition of "orality" refers to the spoken word for communication. In folklore studies, orality means an art or act of speaking, singing, or chanting. In the field of orality studies, orality has been used in a general fashion to describe the structures of consciousness found in cultures

2. See Ulo Valk, "The Quest for Meaning in Folklore and Belief Narrative Studies (with Special Reference to Assam)," in *Orality: The Quest for Meanings* (Zothanchhingi: Partridge Publishing India, 2016).

that are unfamiliar with technologies of writing. Orality relates to the thoughts and verbal expressions of preliterate peoples concerning their worldviews and lifeworlds. According to Walter J. Ong, a pioneering scholar in the field, orality takes two forms: "primary" orality refers to thought and its verbal expression within cultures that are totally untouched by the knowledge of writing or print; "secondary" orality is the new orality sustained by writing, print media, and various electronic devices. Secondary orality is oral culture defined by written and printed words, but is made possible by narrations through audio-visual technologies.[3]

Since the elements of primary orality do not vanish completely in secondary orality, Ong classifies another orality called "oral residue," or "residual orality." He defines this orality as remnants, legacy, or influence of a predominantly oral culture carried over into the written realm. Ong is of the view that residual orality is how many cultures experience the equilibrium in which writing and mass illiteracy have coexisted for centuries. Nevertheless, it is realised that the epistemological significance of orality is more than the written texts, since they turn living thoughts dwelling in the human mind into mere objects in the physical world, thereby weakening the powers of mind and of memory by making people rely on what is written rather than what is remembered. Though balance between the spoken and written words contributed to the cultural and intellectual vitality of various communities in the past, we see true knowledge emerging only from a relationship between active human minds. Therefore, since speech is inherently an oral event based on human relationships, it is more dynamic than written text.[4]

The term "orality" is new in Boro scholarship. Hitherto, phrases like oral tradition, folk tradition, oral narrative, and folk narrative have been buzz words in the field of folklore studies, denoting folktales, songs, and proverbs. The conceptual meaning of the term "orality" can be traced back to Sidney Endle who, a century back, used the ethnic term *khourang* for "folktale" for the first time. Other indigenous scholars like Bhaben Narzee and M. M. Brahma have used the term *solo batha* (ordinary short story). One of the leading scholars of Boro literature, Anil Boro, uses the words *mith* (myth), *solo* (story), *subung solo* (peoples' story), and *gwjam solo* (old story).[5] The common characteristic in these ethnic terms is the "orality," or orally spoken words of the speaker.

3. Walter Ong, *Orality and Literacy: The Technologizing of the Word*, 2nd ed. (London: Routledge, 2002).

4. Ong argues that, unlike a person, a text cannot respond to a question; it will just keep saying the same thing over and over again, no matter how often it is refuted. Ong, *Orality and Literacy*, 78–79.

5. Anil Kumar Boro, *A History of Boro Literature* (Guwahati: Sahitya Akademi, 2010).

The term *khourang* used by Endle makes clear what orality means. He avoided the word *radab*, which relates to news, information, or message, because it does not imply communication by a person directly, whereas *khourang* signifies a live, oral communication brought and announced by a speaker or messenger. In other words, there is no live performance in *radab*, but *khourang* signifies a living demonstration resulting in hearers having something to receive and cheer about. The word itself may be derived from roots meaning "mouth" and "voice," so that this is a message told by a person not as mere information but with emotion and tone of voice. There are elements of secondary orality as well as residual orality in Boro society, yet primary orality describes the reality which remains present today. So in this chapter, "Boro orality" signifies the folklores, folksongs, proverbs, and so on which remain prevalent and are widely used.

Theoretical developments in the field of oral traditions have resulted in valuable studies of the cultures of various communities around the world. A wide range of new and alternative approaches employed to study folk narratives have even helped to recover oral traditions and unearth a host of meanings lying within them. As a result, the quest for meaning in orality has emerged as a significant trend among scholars in recent times. Some of the innovative approaches include the Finnish historic-geographic method and the age-area hypothesis which focus on documenting the spread of traditional tales; the cultural approach that emphasises oral tradition as an information system enabling encoded cultural meanings within a society; the structuralist approach which treats oral tradition as revealing the underlying, universal structure of the human mind; and the psychoanalytic approach in which oral tradition becomes a symbolic projection of unconscious desires.[6] Finally and most important is the *ethnopoetic approach* which emerged as a counter to arbitrary, intellectualist theories and stresses specific local contexts and the

---

6. The work of Finnish folk poetry researcher Julius Leopold Frederick Krohn is described in Christine Goldberg, "The Historic-Geographic Method: Past and Future," *Journal of Folklore Research* 21, no. 1 (April 1984): 1–18. See also D. Dell Hymes, "In Vain I Tried to Tell You," in *Essays in Native-American Ethnopoetics* (Philadelphia: University of Pennsylvania Press, 1981); D. Dell Hymes, *Now I Only Know So Far: Essays in Ethnopoetics* (Lincoln: University of Nebraska Press, 2003); Dennis Tedlock, "Ethnopoetics," in *Folklore, Cultural Performance and Popular Entertainments*, ed. Richard Bauman (New York: Oxford University Press, 1992): 81–85; Dennis Tedlock, *Finding the Center: Narrative Poetry of the Zuni Indians* (New York: Lincoln, 1978); Dennis Tedlock, *The Spoken Word and the Work of Interpretation* (Philadelphia: University of Pennsylvania Press, 1983); and Paul Kroskrity and Anthony Webster, eds, *The Legacy of Del Hymes; Ethnopoetics, Narrative Inequality and Voice* (Bloomington: Indiana University Press, 2015); Anthony Webster, *Intimate Grammars: An Ethnography of Navajo Poetry* (Tucson: University of Arizona Press, 2015).

importance of the “native’s point of view” within each particular culture. This approach significantly moves the focus from text to context with a strong emphasis on performance through gestures, laughter, sighs, and so on. The ethnopoetic approach insists that the documentation or translation of a text must necessarily encapsulate its living performance. According to ethnopoetic theorists, the significance of orality lies not simply in the “contents,” but in rhetorical power, so that meaningfulness arises not merely from words but from the rhythms of linguistic patterning and performance. Consequently, there is always a distortion of aesthetic beauty and poetic sensibility when folk narratives are textualized, even more so if they are translated into another language. In the process of translation, poetic distortion occurs, and the attempt to make quality translations by using standard language results in the whole beauty of the poetic tradition being lost. Such distortion and discrimination can be seen even in the work of linguists and anthropologists, and recently informed ethnopoetics suggests the crucial ways in which attention to voice and narrative inequality can be addressed by attending to texts collected by previous generations.

Besides the approaches of Western scholars are methods initiated by indigenous researchers seeking to understand tribal peoples’ oral narratives. In particular, scholars from Northeast India have adopted alternative approaches beyond Western paradigms. Oral traditions have been approached from fresh perspectives in order to deal with issues such as identity politics, gender and class issues, race, ethnicity, and ecology. Scholars such as Desmond Kharmawphlang see folk narratives as preservers of traditional wisdom and culture and as identity markers. In addition, the feminist approach has recently challenged male dominance, both within the traditions themselves and in the scholarly reading of those traditions. Scholars like Esther Syiem, Temsula Ao, and Margaret Ch. Zama have reread and deconstructed the male paradigms inherent within the oral narratives of indigenous cultures. For example, the oral poetry of the Mizos contains folk songs attributed to female composers, one of whom is said to have been buried alive by traditional authorities because they feared that she would not leave any songs for future generations to compose. We also find female presence in Boro folktales and songs sung at festivals. Such songs offer a wide spectrum of subtle female vocabulary and express women’s concerns and anxieties in playful and humorous fashions. Women who have often been dominated, silenced, and marginalized by men express their protest through the folksongs of oral traditions.

Orality and the Boro Community

The Boro people possess a treasure of oral traditions reflecting the great wisdom of their ancestors. This treasure is a conglomeration of mystery, myth, and reality and can be divided into religious and social categories. The former deal with the creation of the universe, the original human beings, gods and goddesses, and ghosts and spirits, while the latter is related to group identity, history, culture, and social life. This oral tradition took pure speech form until the late nineteenth century when J. D. Anderson, the British administrator turned anthropologist, and Sidney Endle, an administrator turned missionary, initiated the recording of some of these oral traditions into text form. Anderson was a member of the Indian Civil Service from 1873 until 1900. Beside his administrative work, he devoted himself to various forms of social reformation in the Boro rural areas. He travelled in the Mangaldai district of Assam, met Boro people, spent time among them, and collected their folk narratives, translating them into English and publishing them as "A Collection of Kachari Folk Tales and Rhymes" in 1895, which gave Boro oral traditions a documentary form for the first time.

Endle was a pastor who preached Christianity among the Boros in the district of Darrang in Assam. His sense of humour attracted the rural Boro people, and it was said he could preach with ease and eloquence in Boro and other Assamese languages. He mingled with the people and acquired knowledge of their culture, religion, customs, and rituals and translated and published folktales and songs which were sung during festivals at harvest times.[7] Boro scholars recognise that had Anderson and Endle not taken the initiative to collect and translate the contents of Boro orality in textual form at this early period, much would probably have been lost completely.

Notwithstanding the importance and impact of textualization, Boros for centuries have found their distinct identity and life in orality. Their religion, laws and customs, and social and domestic lives are preserved not in written documents but by orality and performance. Their comprehensive orality includes beliefs relating to the origin of the world and humankind, birth, death, birds and animals, and folk songs and wisdom sayings closely connected to socioreligious beliefs, customs, and practices, all transmitted from generation to generation in oral forms and through performance. The various genres of

---

7. The emergence of "Boroni Fisa O Aiyen" in 1915 by the *Habraghat Bodo Sanmilani* (Bodo Student Union) and the first Bodo magazine were due to the inspiration of Anderson and Endle.

Boro orality have been classified into subcategories as follows: myth, legend, folktale, folksong, and proverb. We will explore each of these categories.

Myth is one of the most important genres of Boro prose narrative used to explain cosmology and the supernatural world, together with religious beliefs and traditions presented in story form as having occurred in a certain period of time in a previous age. In common with tribal people around the world, the Boro people have their own myth concerning the creation of the world. It relates how the high God, known as *Aham Guru* (Good Teacher), first created birds, then formed the earth from soil retrieved from a watery chaos, bringing into being the earth with "hills, plains, rivers and ditches." Human beings emerge from two eggs and wished to gain access to heaven, but they discover this is only possible "for people free from sin." The myth contains references to "the noise of quarrel on earth" and the human search for "enough food." So the Boro creation story has parallels to the biblical narrative: both the reality of sin and suffering and the quest for redemption and wholeness are present from the beginning.[8]

Legend is a branch of prose narrative which takes three forms: *religious* legends concern gods and heroes related to religious rituals; *etiological* legends are about the origin of things, the creation of the world and human beginnings; *historical* legends explain prehistory and tell the story of Bodo kings, chieftains, and heroes and heroines. Such legends play a vital role in Bodo society and history, illustrating patriotism, love, and respect for the Bodo nation and culture through acts of heroism, and they continue to inspire the mass of Bodo people today.

For example, a legend concerning *Birgwshri sikla* (flying girl), also known as *Theng phakhri* (swift-footed runner), who was a *mauzadar*, or "revenue collector" of the Bodo community during the British regime, is depicted as a courageous and straightforward woman.[9] Her job was to collect revenues and deposit them annually along with valuable goods to the government of British India. There was a rule that if *mauzadars* failed to deposit the fixed amount along with the valuable goods, the British would impose penalties upon them.

8. The myth referred to here is published in Kameswar Brahma, *A Study of Socio-Religious Beliefs, Practices and Ceremonies of the Bodos* (Calcutta: Punthi Pustak, 1992), 118–21.

9. Indira Goswami, author of the novel *The Bronze Sword of Thengphakhri Tehsildar*, translated and introduced by Aruni Kashap (New Delhi: Zubaan, 2013) said that the story of a "fierce feminist character who fought against the dominant powers and sacrificed her life for the sake of her people which no other woman could do remains as living inspiration," viii. During the Bodoland movement for a separate state begun in the 1980s, people have invoked the name of Birgwsri to challenge women to support demands for justice.

Birgwshri objected to this rule and determined not to collect and pay the revenue. She found that colonial taxes were squeezing the poor Boro farmers, especially in a drought-hit year. As a result she and her people were declared defaulters, and she was forced to pay the arrears. When she refused to supply the revenue, there was a clash between her and the British authorities which resulted in Boro resistance to British soldiers. Birgwshri fought bravely but had to flee for her life and took shelter behind a small hillock. When she came out of hiding to find water in a nearby stream, she was shot dead by British soldiers.

People living in the area where this incident took place began naming the hill after the heroine, so that today it is known in a Sanskritized form as Bageswshari hill and has a temple named Bageswari Mandir. It is said that the sword of Birgwshri was found by a priest, and believing that it belonged to a deity, he erected a temple and placed the sword at its centre. Today people from diverse religious backgrounds come to worship the Bageswari goddess. The Boro people consider this incident an example of a legend becoming history because in the spirit of legendary female heroines, Bageswari defended her own people against an imperial power and herself became a heroine whose actions continue to inspire Boro people in their demands for human rights and justice.

Folktale is another branch of prose narrative which includes the origins, migration, and settlement of the Boros as told by people in the past and handed down orally from generation to generation. These tales are amusing to listeners since they employ language of romance and fun, but at the same time they are rich in instruction and edifying for relational or community living. They also deploy imaginative natural and supernatural elements. It is important to observe that the impact of folktales depends upon the artistic skill of the storyteller who narrates them using facial expressions, body language, and emotions. Often the moral of the tale is left unstated but implied so that listeners can reach the right conclusion themselves.

Folksong is yet another genre with rich significance for harmonious living. These songs too are romantic and humorous expressions of deep concepts or inner feelings of human life such as beauty, love, joy, and happiness as well as suffering and agony. Various subgenres within folk songs include love songs, play songs, workplace songs, devotional songs, and children's songs, all sung at specific seasons and times. Mohini Mahan Brahma, a towering Boro writer, in his work *Folk Songs of the Bodos* classified the collection into various subdivisions including patriotism and valour, songs of the soil, nursery rhymes, the course of love, the gift of humour, prayer, and ritual.[10]

---

10. M. M. Brahma, *Folk Songs of the Boros* (Gauhati: Gauhati University, 1960).

Folksongs still echo in Boro villages, and the pastures, plains, meadows, and harvest fields reverberate with song. While working in the fields, Boro men and women tell humorous stories and sing songs of valour and humour. Women sing as they weave various designs on the cloth on their looms. Romantic songs are sung by boys and girls dialectically, and Boro marriage ceremonies are musical affairs where many songs are performed. There are songs associated with the granary and the cowshed, and underlying many lyrics is the importance of land, nature, and animals, recognising them as the source of sustenance. This recognition is especially clear in songs related to harvests, called *bwisagu*, the celebration of nature's bounty and beauty. At these festivals people express their joy and happiness by dancing and singing poetic songs describing the beauty of both nature and loved ones using words and expressions of adoration and the glorification of youth. People pour out their hearts both in expressing sorrow and frustration and in the renewal of life through merrymaking.

Proverbs and Riddles are important culture-specific subgenres of Boro orality containing deep philosophy and reflecting the worldview and lifeworld of the community. These sayings can be categorised as wisdom sayings since they express the inner truth and meanings of life's reality through ordinary things and use words and language in metaphorical or symbolic ways. Proverbs in particular are very terse metaphoric statements on various aspects of life and are known by Boro people as *bathra bhao*, wordplay or act or performance of words. Proverbs and riddles are used as indirect and impersonal ways of communicating something which has direct and personal meaning and instruction for individuals or the community.

The fact that proverbs, riddles, and sayings are used to convey indirect meanings and lessons results in non-Boro speakers, and sometimes Boro people themselves, experiencing difficulty in understanding such sayings. Here are some examples:

> *Sikhaoni salaia khanda*, literally "tongue of a thief is half," means a thief can neither tell the truth nor lie convincingly. This saying is used during arguments to judge the truth or untruth of a person's words.
>
> *Wngkharnai khansria happhina*, "earthworm which comes out of ground never enters back again," expresses the firmness of a speaker's word or justification for a word or action and unwillingness to retract it.

> *Adaya kiyw bajwia gadlayw*, "elder brother excretes in open space but sister-in-law steps on it," refers to an irresponsible person who does things wrong, but someone innocent bears the consequences and is held responsible.

The Significance of Boro Names

The Boro people are known by names which relate to stories of nature-oriented social responsibility. It is believed that these surnames were created by Mwnsing-sing-Bwrai – one of the original human persons in the creation myth – to bring social order when people in mythical time lived in a chaotic atmosphere of social irresponsibility. There is a story that tells of a great convention of Boro society held to assign specific work and duties to people under the leadership of the first human being, Mwnsingsing Bwrai, who had come down from heaven to convene the convention which strangely lasted for twelve years! At the end of the convention, the people were segregated into groups called *hari* or *ari*, according to the specific work or duties they were to be engaged in.

For example, some were to be engaged in worship, or a worshipping group, and were named *sorgoyari* (*swrgw* + *hari*), the "heavenly folk." Those engaged in cultivation and having responsibility for land distribution and solving any disputes related to landholdings were called *baiswmutiari/ basumatari (bwiswmata* + *hari*), the "mother earth folk." Similarly, *narzari* (*narzi* + *hari*), meaning "jute leaf folk," were the ones who worked in vegetation, or the collection of *narzi* and its distribution during funeral rites, since dried jute leaves are displayed as a mark of the cut off with the death of a person. The *mwsahari/ muchahari/ mosahari*, or "tiger folk," were those who were believed to be entrusted with the duty of safeguarding the people and their domestic animals from the danger of attack by tigers. *Daimari* (big river + *hari*) were "river folk," while *owari/wari* (*owa* + *hari*) were "bamboo folk." Daimaris were people who lived by large river banks and survived by fishing, while Owaris had the occupation of collecting and supplying bamboo in large quantities for religious festivals and other social conventions, and Hajwaris were people whose habitat was in the hills. All other surnames are associated with people's occupations and duties within the society, all of which were very much oriented toward nature and its care. An important aspect of this social structure is that there is no hierarchy visible among these people groups even today. Despite the different duties and responsibilities assigned to them, these are purely surnames designating functions without any religious or social distinction or hierarchy. All people groups follow one language and culture and maintain equal identity and status.

Meanings and Values of Boro Orality

We note that the study of the oral cultures of the Northeast Indian tribes pioneered by colonial ethnographers has been very negative concerning their religious traditions and cultures.[11] With Western parameters they considered them to be primitive, irrational, and uncivilized and to indicate the need for Western education and the power of the gospel. These ethnographers' onto-theologically driven Western thought utterly failed to understand and interpret the nuanced meanings of the deep cosmological worldview, beliefs, and values inherent within local cultures and socioreligious practices. However, unlike the case in other communities in Northeast India, the distorted view in anthropological and colonial reports did not make much impact on the Boro community. Although some of their oral traditions are steadily disappearing, Boro oral culture remains a living reality in its own right, including its highly artistic power and beautiful verbal expressions and performances. The majority of the Boro population today conduct most of their cultural affairs by oral means which display inherent philosophical and psychosocial dynamics which play a great epistemological role in the society. The compositions and expressions of Boro orality transcend mere entertainment and are both challenging and inspiring to the minds and emotions of the people; the language and rhythms are socially challenging and psychologically important. Boro orality expresses the people's love, ecstasy, joy, and happiness as well as physical and psychological pain, fatigue, sorrow, anxiety, anger, disgust, and frustration. To witness folksongs and folktales being sung and told in work places and fields during pruning, cultivating, weaving, or constructing roads or houses is fascinating and demonstrates the ways in which this tradition brings joy and relief from physical pain and boosts the determination of the toiling masses of labourers to complete their work.

However, it must be stressed that Boro orality is truly communitarian and participatory in nature, springing from a context of collective situational thinking on day-to-day life issues. Perhaps the fundamental principle of Boro orality concerns the discovery of truth and the process of decision making on any issue through communitarian and participatory processes in which

11. Colonial administrators turned anthropologists across Northeast India included J. H. Hutton, J. P. Mills, John Shakespeare, T. H. Lewin, and N. E. Parry among others.

community members share in intimate, empathetic, and communal association with each other. Everything is of concern and interest to all members of a community, and those who do not internalise the instructive oral traits of Boro culture face social isolation. The communitarian concepts embedded within oral tradition go beyond anthropocentric views of the world, extending to human relations with nature, creation, and spirit beings.

Being the social product of the community, Boro orality serves as a means of communal admonition and guidance, bringing people into close communion through the practice of beliefs and values inherent in daily life. It can also be a *social control mechanism and a socializing agent,* upholding social organizations, customary laws, religious practices, and ethical values. While being a wealthy repository of the mythical, legendary, and historical past, Boro orality also provides examples and values for social order and sustaining the community. It educates people regarding life's realities and their moral responsibilities, and its performative character makes it a powerful instrument in boosting the morale of individuals and encouraging behavioural change.

By being *combative* in nature and *agonistic* in expression, Boro orality can act as an agent of social protest and change. Because the Boro people face a highly polarized world and the realities of the tensions between good and evil, virtue and vice, friends and foes, the powerful and the powerless, and villains and heroes, much of the content of oral tradition is combative, enabling the articulation of social concerns, the raising of dissent and protest, and the demands to redress the social evils in the society. In sum, Boro orality mirrors Boro society as it plays a key role in establishing and sustaining the *history and unique identity of the Boro nation.*

To modern minds imbued with the so-called enlightened Western epistemological lenses and related normative hermeneutics, orality cannot be preserved in a world in which literacy and the entire range of technologies associated with it seem to be everywhere dominant. Although the Boro people do possess literature, they remain dependent upon the oral traditions, and their world continues to be made meaningful through orality. Their traditional socioreligious systems and cultural practices remain well preserved by means of performative transmissions. As we have seen, the social and cultural life of the people, especially in the villages which are governed by unwritten laws and guidelines used by village councils under the leadership of headmen, are sustained by orality articulated through inherited meaning-making modes with rhetorical and rhythmic power. Whereas Western theories of meaning highlight the interpretation of written texts, Boro orality, it may be claimed, *is the expression of meaning itself.* It springs from meaningful life and creates ordered individual existence and a community living by shared meanings reiterated orally and passed on from one generation to another by speech and performance. As human beings are always meaning-seeking and meaning-creating beings, Boros have since time immemorial been on a quest for meaning for life in everything, and those meanings continue to be upheld and transmitted in various oral forms of expression. The words of Walter Ong may be applied to the experience of the Boro people and their oral traditions: "Oral cultures indeed produce powerful and beautiful verbal performances of high artistic and human worth, which are no longer even possible once writing has taken possession of the psyche."[12]

Conclusion

Perhaps the distinctions often made between oral and written traditions, or between non-theological and theological worldviews, treating these epistemologies within an evolutionary framework by which orality is transcended as being irrational and primitive, need to be abandoned. In fact traditions of interpretation developed around written texts are determined by the truth which emerges from oral contexts. In other words, it is not textual traditions which determine the value and meaning of orality, but rather oral traditions which underlie and are foundational to written texts. Those foundational human traditions are centred around the conception of God as immanent and the interconnectedness of all beings and things. The Boro folk domain creates an understanding of the world in which the interrelatedness and coexistence of God, spirits, and all created beings are taken for granted. In such a culture the concept of personal salvation apart from the community is inconceivable since the entire understanding of life and reality is focused on social solidarity through events such as births and deaths and modes of communal life together. Traditional beliefs connect the past to the present and the individual to the whole community, thereby finding existential meaning in life together.

Boro orality has thus played a great role of guardianship of the peace, harmony, social cohesion, and communitarian society. The philosophical and psychosocial dynamics between orality and society have enabled the Boro people to maintain their unique identity amid the hegemonic threats posed by the dominant cultures in a globalised age. With its cosmoplastic, world-

12. Ong, *Orality and Literacy*, 14. He wrote further on the challenges of orality in "Before Textuality: Orality and Interpretation," *Oral Tradition* 3, no. 3 (1988): 259–69.

making power, Boro orality has defined and sustained this people as a whole, and its rich epistemological potentials and ontological relevance suggest that it presents a challenge to the presuppositions underlying the modern world. Perhaps the time is ripe for an epistemological transformation and historical re-rooting, since the story others have narrated and the history others have written concerning the Boros are neither their story nor their history!

For further information on this topic, see the following:

Arjun Basumatary, *Bodo Christians: The Bodo Movement and Nation Building* (Delhi: ISPCK, 2017).

Shyam Kumar Basumatary, *Keeping Faith: An Integrative Model of Christian Religious Education in Postcolonial Perspective* (Delhi: ISPCK, 2017).

Songram Basumatary, *Ethnicity and Tribal Theology: Problems and Prospects for Peaceful Co-existence in Northeast India* (Bern: Peter Lang, 2014).

Kameswar Brahma, *A Study of Socio-Religious Beliefs, Practices and Ceremonies of the Bodos* (Calcutta: Punthi Pustak, 1992).

Zothanchhingi Khiangte, *Orality: The Quest for Meanings* (Zothanchhingi: Partridge Publishing India, 2016).

Walotemjen Basumatary and Songram Basumatary, *Your History Is Not Our Story: Re-imagining Colonial Historiography of Tribals and Christianity in North East India* (New Delhi: Christian World Imprints, 2019).

7

The Inculturation of Christianity among the Khasi People of Meghalaya State

Fabian Lyngdoh

This chapter presents a brief discussion on the present status of inculturation of the Christian faith in the Khasi and Jaintia Hills in the State of Meghalaya, India, with special reference to the Catholic Church. At the outset I would like to make it clear that this chapter does not stand on the point of view that the Christian faith introduced by Western missionaries among the tribals of Northeast India has become redundant today since Christianity is now declining in the West. Instead, I argue that Christianity is neither Western nor Eastern, but universal and ever relevant through time and space as it is enfleshed in peoples' lifeworlds.

In the past, Christianity was regarded as a "finished product" in the Western form with theological and political Eurocentrism.[1] The "Church took it for granted that there was a single, universal culture of humanity, the perfection of which was deemed to be Christianity in its Western, Latin form," and as far as Catholics are concerned, it was only in the twentieth century at the Second Vatican Council and in the subsequent assemblies of the synod of

1. Joseph Pothenpurakal, "Inculturation in India," paper presented at the Oriens-SHTC Seminar on Inculturation in Northeast India, Oriens Theological College, Shillong, 27 August 2009. Fr. Joseph Pothenpurakal blog, https://jputhen.blogspot.com/2009/08/.

bishops that "cultural pluralism" was accepted in the Catholic Church, together with inculturation as a demand of evangelization.[2]

Theological concern today centres on the concept of world Christianity which relates to the multiplicity of indigenous responses to the Christian gospel[3] and the need for inculturation to render the Christian faith relevant through time and space. According to the Federation of Asian Bishops Conference (FABC), inculturation is understood as the deep and mutually enriching encounter between the gospel and the people of a particular culture and tradition. It consists not only in the expression of the gospel and the Christian faith through the cultural medium, but also includes experiencing, understanding, and appropriating the gospel through the cultural resources of a people.[4] Our concern here is with the inculturation of Christianity in the tribal cultures of Northeast India.

Tribal Culture

Tribal societies are usually identified on the basis of common names and languages that distinguish one tribe from another. They are generally endogamous groups, organized on the basis of clan and kinship systems and indigenous political organizations. Their cultural traditions evolve and are confined within a definite geographical territory which is considered as the gift of God or the ancestors. Tribal societies are egalitarian in nature and have a strong sense of unity and a haunting collective sense of the need for defence and protection against physical and cultural invasions. Each individual's dignity and identity is respected, but always under the umbrella of the collective identity in which individualism has no place.

Tribal peoples strongly believe in the existence of the spiritual realm where spiritual beings exist and the spirits of the ancestors continue to live, and religion is the means by which their relationship with this spiritual realm is conducted. Religion stands at the core of their culture as it is an agency that

---

2. *New Catholic Encyclopedia* (Washington, DC: Catholic University of America, 2003). https://www.encyclopedia.com/religion/encyclopedias-almanacs-transcripts-and-maps inculturation-theology Accessed on 10 October 2019.

3. On this see, Lamin Sanneh, *Whose Religion is Christianity? The Gospel Beyond the West* (Grand Rapids, MI: Eerdmans, 2003), 22–23; See also "World Christianity," Wikipedia, https://en.wikipedia.org/wiki/World_Christianity, accessed 4 April 2019.

4. F. Fernandez, "A Process of Growth of the Church in the Khasi and Jaintia Hills," in *He Taught: A Festschrift in Honour of Sylvanus Sngi Lyngdoh, SDB.*, eds. G. Kattuppallil and Jose Varickkasseril (Shillong: Vendrame Institute Publications, 1996), 365–76.

provides security against, or negotiation with, natural and spiritual forces that are more powerful than human beings. However, there is no sharp distinction between sacred and profane, religious and secular in their day-to-day living. Hence, they have a filial relationship with the land and solidarity with nature which forms part of their economic, social, cultural, and religious identity.

These characteristics determine and make up the cultural traditions of tribal peoples. Different kinds of customs may evolve in tribal societies according to different natural and historical circumstances, but they may not differ much in their underlying cultural traditions. It is within the context of these cultural traditions that inculturation is to take place among the tribal peoples. For a long time tribal people uncritically accepted Christianity with doctrines which were far removed from the concerns of their day-to-day life.[5] The majority of Christians in India belong to tribal communities,[6] but their cultural traditions and contemporary experiences have not been made a major part of theological reflection in India.[7] If theology truly aims at transformative praxis which leads to the establishment of the kingdom of God based on justice, equality, kinship and peace, then we see it already operative in tribal societies. The whole church has much to gain from integrating tribal experience and wisdom within the mosaic of Christian life and theology.[8] Hence, it is imperative today to relook at the core values of traditional tribal worldviews that are in tune with gospel values while not losing sight of the newer realities of the present day.[9]

Inculturation of Hinduism among the Khasis

To have a better understanding of the inculturation of the Christian faith among the Khasis, it is necessary to look into the inculturation of Hinduism in the precolonial and premodern period. Not long before the coming of the

---

5. M. G. Kariapuram, "Tribal Hermeneutics for a Contextual Theology," in *He Taught: A Festschrift in Honour of Sylvanus Sngi Lyngdoh, SDB.*, eds. G. Kattuppallil and Jose Varickkasseril (Shillong: Vendrame Institute Publications, 1996), 327–52.

6. "Khasi Tribe Erects Monuments of Faith," UCA NEWS Union of Catholic Asian News Limited (26 July 1998), https://www.ucanews.com/story-archive/?post_name=/1998/07/27/khasi-tribe-erects-monuments-of-faith&post_id=11837.

7. J. Kannanaikal, "Scheduled Castes and Scheduled Tribes and the Church in India," in *The Catholic Community of India: Towards the Twenty First Century* (Bombay: Report of the National Convention of Catholics, 2–5 June 1989), 166.

8. M. G. Kariapuram, "Tribal Hermeneutics for a Contextual Theology," in *He Taught: A Festschrift in Honour of Sylvanus Sngi Lyngdoh, SDB.*, eds. G. Kattuppallil and Jose Varickkasseril (Shillong: Vendrame Institute Publications, 1996), 348.

9. A. D'Souza, Lalnghakthuami, and Pangernungba Kechu, eds., *Family and Clan in North East India: Reflections* (Guwahati: North Eastern Social Research Centre, 2015).

British, Hindu deities had been incorporated into the community religions of many traditional Khasi states called *Hima* or *Raid*. The cult of the Hindu god Viswakarma, known among the Khasis as *Biskoram,* was more widespread than other Hindu deities, but as Khasi society is matrilineal, goddesses were more widely incorporated than gods. The cult of Laxmi, known in Khasi as *Lukhmi*, *Lakhmi*, or *Lukhimai*, is found in the religions of several traditional village states in the Ri Bhoi District of Meghalaya, called the *Raids*, where it is linked with the cultivation of rice. The cults of Kali and Durga are found in the Jaintia Hills area, where Hinduism has been deeply incorporated in community religions as well as in individual families. There have also been human sacrifices in some parts of the Khasi and Jaintia Hills in connection with the worship of the Hindu goddess Kali.

In Raid Iapngar, one of numerous traditional Khasi village states, human sacrifices were offered to a god called *Baribhai-Saribhai*. In the traditional religion of the *Dimasa Kachari*, another of the tribal communities in Northeast India, the Hindu god Shiva is worshipped by the name *Brai Sibrai*.[10] In fact, this name is similar to *Bhairava*, a fierce manifestation of Shiva associated with annihilation. So it seems that human sacrifice practiced among the Khasis was connected with the Hindu god *Bhairava*.

Khasis also offered animal sacrifices to a goddess of violence called *Ramchandi*, and when they prepared for war, they smeared their weapons with the blood of sacrificial animals so that their weapons would become bloodthirsty and perform well in battle. According to oral tradition, this goddess was said to eat up members of the community if they failed to perform the required sacrifices. The name *Ramchandi* is similar to *Chandika* which signifies the violent aspect of the Hindu goddess Parvati. Hence the inculturation of Hinduism in Khasi traditional beliefs and practices is evident in the Khasi and Jaintia Hills long before the advent of British rule and the introduction of Christianity.

Influence of Hinduism and Christianity on Khasi Thought Patterns

Christian missionaries came to the Khasis of Meghalaya early in the nineteenth century, independent of the colonial policy but in many ways facilitated by the new political and administrative developments. The first mission among the tribe was the English Baptist Mission of Serampore, followed by the Welsh Calvinistic Methodist Mission which commenced activities in 1841.

10. J. V. Haokip, *Mythology of North East India* (Shillong: DBCIC, 2011), 86.

Catholics had been in the region much earlier, but their formal mission activity commenced in 1890 through the German Salvatorian Missionaries.[11] Today, Christianity has become the religion of the majority of the Khasi people, and at present Presbyterians and Catholics are the most dominant Christian sects in the Khasi and Jaintia Hills. However, a significant number of the Khasis have not adopted Christianity and are said to follow their traditional religion.

Toward the end of the nineteenth century, some educated Khasi leaders were apprehensive that the culture and identity of the tribe would be overwhelmed by modern influences, especially by the spread of Christianity. This feeling was to some extent instigated by the Christian missionaries and their local followers who demonized Khasi beliefs and religious practices. This demonization led to the formation of the *Seng Khasi* in 1899, an organization of Khasi non-Christians who had the objective of preserving and protecting the Khasi culture and traditional religion.

However, it is obvious that Hinduism and Christianity have both deeply influenced Khasi thought and practice, even among those who claim that they practice the Khasi traditional religion. In reaction to Christian missions, Jeebon Roy, one of the earliest leaders of the Khasi renaissance, was inclined to interpret Khasi religion in line with Hinduism. In his book *Ka Kitab Shaphang Uwei u Blei* (1900), translated by Bijoya Sawian in 2005 as *About One God*, Jeebon Roy suggests that religion among the Khasis includes the performance of rites and rituals in every clan which is called *niam*. But true religion, according to him, is not *niam* but "dharma" which grows and develops slowly in our hearts.[12] Jeebon Roy taught that when the soul leaves the body, the person goes to the house of God and merges with divine consciousness.[13] However, according to Khasi religious thought, departed souls do not go to the house of God but meet their own ancestors, and with them eat betel nut *ha dwar u Blei* (in the portico of the house of God). This belief implies that a human soul does not merge into divine consciousness but retains personal entity as an individual soul in communion with the spirits of his or her ancestors.

Sib Charan Roy Jaitdkhar, a prominent leader of the *Seng Khasi*, in his book *Ka Niam-Ki-Khasi: Ka Niam Tip-Blei-Tip-Brieu* (*Khasi Religion: A Religion of Knowing God – Knowing Man*) published in 1919, attempts to streamline

11. M. Syiemlieh, "Early Khasi Response to Christian Missions: Challenges, Acceptance and Assertion," *Journal of Humanities and Social Science (IOSR-JHSS)* 14, no. 2 (Jul. – Aug. 2013): 36–43, http://www.iosrjournals.org/iosr-jhss/papers/Vol14-issue2/G01423643.pdf.

12. B. Saiwan, trans., *About One God* (Shillong: Ri Khasi Enterprise, 2005), 56–57.

13. Saiwan, *About One God,* 39.

Khasi religious thought in tune with both Hinduism and Christianity. He propagates the idea that the Khasi concept of *ka sot* means the truth, the eternal being that needs no proof as it is self-evident and cannot be otherwise.[14] The concept of *ka sot* is an adaptation of the Hindu idea of "Sat," which relates to the unchangeable and imperishable truth, which could be called "Being itself." *Chit* is pure consciousness or total awareness, the self-reflection of Sat in itself, while *Ananda* is bliss, the ecstasy of being, or Sat.[15] The Khasi concept of *ka sot* cannot be identified with the Hindu "Sat" since it refers not to a being, but to a system of divinely sanctioned socioreligious code.

Sib Charan Roy says that God is within us, and we are in God.[16] He also taught people that in times of sickness, they should pray to God who resides within the self.[17] But in reality, it is considered taboo for a Khasi to say that God resides within oneself, and this concept is clearly borrowed from the Advaita philosophy of Hinduism. It is also possible to detect the influence of Christianity here since in John 14:17–20 Jesus says, "you will realize that I am in my Father, and you are in me, and I am in you" (v. 20). Sib Charan Roy instructs his followers that when they pray to God, they should not pray in front of other people,[18] which again may be derived from Jesus' words in Matthew 6:6: "But when you pray, go into your room, close the door and pray to your Father, who is unseen." There is no evidence in Khasi tradition of a taboo on praying in front of other people.

Sib Charan Roy taught that God created humankind last, after he had created everything that humankind needs.[19] The influence of the Bible can be seen here, and this concept appears to be adapted from the biblical account of creation (Gen 1:26). But according to Khasi oral tradition, while humankind was created by God, there is no indication of when, where, or how this took place. Humankind's existence is presupposed to be in heaven before the creation of the earth, and it is only when the earth and all things in it were created that they descended down the golden stairs. Sib Charan Roy believed that those persons who are born crippled may have been criminals and oppressors in

14. S. C. Roy Jaitdkhar, *Ka Niam-Ki-Khasi: Ka Niam TipBlei-Tip-Brieu* (Shillong: Ri Khasi Press, 1993 [1919]), vi-vii.

15. A. Ghose, *The Life Divine* (Calcutta: Arya, 1947), 115; M. von Bruck, "Advaita and Trinity: Reflections on the Vedantic and Christian Experience of God with Reference to Buddhist Non-Dualism," Indian Theological Studies 20 (March 1983): 44–45.

16. Jaitdkhar, *Ka Niam-Ki-Khasi*, ii.

17. Jaitdkhar, 70.

18. Jaitdkhar, 70.

19. Jaitdkhar, iv.

their previous lives,[20] a conclusion which must arise from an adaptation of the Hindu concept of the cycle of rebirth and the transmigration of souls. But once again, the traditional Khasis do not believe in the doctrine of rebirth or the transmigration of souls; rather, as we noted previously, they anticipated a post mortem reunion with their ancestors.

Tral Singh Mawthoh, a well-known priest of the Khasi traditional religion who is still practicing today, adopted and successfully put into practice some aspects of the Christian faith. According to Mawthoh, God has given authority to his Son, *u Rangiar-khad*u (sacrificial cock), to be the saviour and redeemer of mankind through his self-sacrifice. It is through *u Rangiar-khad* and his conquest of all the powers of evil that human beings are brought back to peace and unity with God.[21] This idea is clearly an adaptation of the story of Jesus, the Son of God, who conquered Satan through his death and resurrection and thereby reconciled humankind with God. Mawthoh says that the altar of the Khasi traditional religion is founded on three divine realities that God had established: first, of God the Father; second, of the goddess *Hukum* or *Dorbar Blei*; and third, of the sacrificial cock as the Son of God.[22] Here the Christian doctrine of the Holy Trinity is brought into the picture with the Holy Spirit replaced and a traditional goddess introduced. Quite apart from its distortion of Christian teaching, this formulation within a movement intended to preserve Khasi beliefs is also in conflict with the fact that God was never seen by the Khasis as "Father"; neither was the concept of the "Son of God" present in Khasi tradition. In Mawthoh's sacrificial prayers these words always appear: *Long ba la kyrkhu ia phi u Blei* (Blessed be you oh God), yet this expression, although having biblical precedents, contradicts Khasi traditional thought according to which humankind is unworthy of offering blessing to God since blessings can only flow one way, from God to humankind and not from humankind to God.

Mawthoh teaches that humankind's relationship with God is based on *ka Jutang* (covenant) which comprises a series of commandments and which, Mawthoh claims, were part and parcel of the Khasi religion.[23] These commandments commence with the instruction to "honour and love your God, not to take his name in vain, and to worship no other gods." The similarity with the Decalogue given to Moses and recorded in the Bible is striking, and

20. Jaitdkhar, 66.

21. Tral Singh Mawthoh, *Ka Jingai Jingknia: Katkum ka Niam Tynrai jong ki Khun u Hynniewtrep* (Shillong: Galaxy Book Centre, 2018), 1.

22. Mawthoh, *Ka Jingai Jingknia*, 32.

23. Mawthoh, 2.

the parallels continue with reference to a day of rest on which to "celebrate in happiness with me" the command to honour father and mother and to "love and respect fellow human beings." Killing, adultery, theft, false witness, embezzlement, and coveting "what belongs to others" are all identified as practices that are contrary to the love of both God and humankind, so the Mosaic Ten Commandments are clearly reflected in this Khasi covenant given by Mawthoh. Furthermore, the rite of traditional religious sacrifices as practiced and described by Mawthoh is fashioned in line with the Catholic liturgy of the Mass. Tral Singh Mawthoh also says that the doctrine of the original sin committed by the first human parents and inherited by the offspring, along with the teaching that the "wages of sin is death," are part of Khasi traditional religious thought.[24] This inculturation of biblical doctrine into the Khasi religious thought is remarkable considering the fact that Tral Singh Mawthoh is a renowned practicing priest of the Khasi indigenous religion today.

Some Khasi Christian authors have also attempted to interpret the traditional religious thought in relation to the biblical narratives. For example in 1936, Soso Tham, the renowned Khasi poet and ardent follower of the Christian faith, wrote that according to Khasi mythology, in a *dorbar* (council) of all creatures, the cock made a covenant to offer his neck in sacrifice to bear the sins of mankind, and this covenant would last until the coming of the heavenly bird called *u Syiem Simpah Simsong, u Simkaro.* Soso Tham concluded that eternal peace shall reign on earth when the King of Heaven shall trample Satan under his feet.[25]

In 1937, Homiwell Lyngdoh in his book *Ka Niam Khasi* (Khasi religion) says that the purpose of the Khasi religion is to guide and lead the tribe on the right path until the arrival of a superior being who would bear all the sins of mankind and shower abundant grace to bring the Khasi religion to perfection.[26] Homiwell Lyngdoh concluded that the religion of the Khasis is founded on the basis of *apkhmihlynti* (waiting in expectation) for the coming of that superior being, or the saviour of mankind who will lead all human souls to the house of God.[27] Today, a version of this culturally rooted spirit of "waiting in expectation" is being incorporated into the liturgy of the Mass in the Shillong Archdiocese by some Catholic priests. It is evident that these Christian writers intended to refer the expected heavenly bird, or deliverer, to Jesus Christ. But

24. Mawthoh, 138.
25. S. Tham, *Ka Duitara Ksiar* (Shillong: University Press, 1936 [1979]), 26–28.
26. H. Lyngdoh, *Ka Niam k iKhasi* (Shillong: Ri Khasi Book Agency, 1937 [2013]), 15–16.
27. Lyngdoh, *Ka Niam k iKhasi*, 16.

according to Tral Singh Mawthoh, the expression *u Kynrem u Lyndan, u Syntai I bulot* does not refer to a coming deliverer but to a bull, as the proper Khasi religious ritual begins with an inquiry through egg divination followed by the sacrifice of a cock, and finally concludes with the sacrifice of a bull.[28]

Inculturation in the Catholic Church among the Khasis

According to Vincent Kympat, Bishop of Jowai Diocese, the core elements of Khasi spirituality are the centrality of God, the privileged position of sacrifice, the key role of the family (clan), and the pride of place given to prayer. Bishop Kympat believes that Khasi spirituality is already to a great extent theocentric, liturgical, and family and community oriented, and that it connects at many points with the biblical revelation. The Khasi belief in the communion of the living with their departed relatives, whom they believe are still alive, is similar to the Catholic belief in the communion of saints, while in the Khasi matriarchal society, the veneration of Mary the mother of Jesus is easily understood. Hence, according to Bishop Kympat, Khasi spirituality is already fertile soil for the expression of Catholic Christian spirituality.[29]

Fr. Sylvanus Sngi Lyngdoh, a great champion of inculturation among the Khasis, contends that the Catholic Church in Khasi and the Jaintia Hills is deeply rooted in faith and shows the way to inculturate the gospel within tribal traditions. The Khasis traditionally raise stone memorials on significant occasions, and this custom has been incorporated into church architecture and vestments used by the Catholic Church to explain its truths. A tribal Christology recognizes Jesus as the great maternal uncle in this matrilineal society. According to Fr. Sngi, Khasi tradition is a religion of waiting and longing, so people have accepted the Christian faith in large numbers precisely because they see the gospel as a fulfilment of their traditional aspirations and hopes. The first Khasi Archbishop of Shillong, Tarcisius Resto Phanrang, incorporated both Catholic and traditional Khasi symbols in his coat of arms which depicts three stones planted erect, with a flat one in front to signify the Khasi ancestor, and a cross at the centre of the three stones. Archbishop Phanrang explained that the cross symbolizes Christ as the light of the world who comes to enlighten, to purify and strengthen, and to bring the culture

28. Mawthoh, *Ka Jingnai Jinghnia*, 24.

29. V. Kympat, "Khasi Spirituality for Catechesis," in *He Taught: A Festschrift in Honour of Sylvanus Sngi Lyngdoh, SDB*., eds. G. Kattuppallil and Jose Varickkasseril (Shillong: Vendrame Institute Publications, 1996), 378–82.

of the Khasi ancestors to perfection.[30] Today the symbol of a cock is used in religious vestments, monoliths have been raised, and cultural dances are being organized in almost every Catholic local community. Indigenous thought patterns in prayers and ceremonies on the occasions of births and the deaths of the faithful have been introduced, including an important element of Khasi religious practice whereby permission is asked of God before commencing any important function, whether in social or personal life.[31] Fr. Sngi Lyngdoh has been instrumental in coining new words in the Christian liturgy rooted in the Khasi language and tradition. He has also identified the seven sacraments of the Catholic Church with seven sacred practices at crucial points in human experience within the traditional religion of the Khasis.

Some of these elements of inculturation have found their way into the official hymn and liturgy book in the Archdiocese of Shillong called *Ka Lynti Bneng* (The Way to Heaven). The Eucharistic prayer of the Archdiocese of Shillong is formulated in the Khasi thought pattern: *Shihajarnguh Blei Trai Kynrad najrong natbian* (A thousand worship God Lord above and below), *ko Nongthaw Nonghbuh* (the Designer and Creator), *ko Nongsambynta, Nongbuhbynta* (the Allocator and Regulator), *ko Nongsei ia ka lonrynieng longrta* (the Begetter of human life), *ko Balah ko Baiai* (the Omnipotent One), *shikhrum ka bneng shtyllup ka pyrthei* (throughout the basement of heaven, the whole wide world).

The Catholic Church is more liberal about inculturation than the Presbyterian Church. However since the 1990s, the Presbyterian Church has also been alive to the questions thrown at it by young Khasis, both clergy and lay people. This tradition too has been required to respond to the question, "Why won't the church express its faith in local culture?" Khasi traditional musical instruments, which were for a long time not permitted in church worship services, have come to be used more and more in secondary church events or in synod meetings if not during the main worship services. Individual pastors have taken the lead in adding local colour to church ceremonies, but the inculturation of the Christian faith in the Khasi and Jaintia Hills has not happened without challenges.

Not only have churches been hesitant, but as already mentioned, the *Seng Khasi* movement of the non-Christian Khasi intelligentsia opposes the spread of Christianity which they regard as a force threatening to destroy

30. "Khasi Tribe Erects Monuments of Faith."

31. Fernandez, "Process of Growth," 369.

the Khasi religion and culture.[32] The leaders of the *Seng Khasi* and a similar movement, *Sein Raij*, have moved to consider Khasi Christians as people who have forfeited their Khasi identity. There have also been debates, contesting, and strong reactions by people who affirm traditional religion against the contextualized theology and worship of Khasi Christianity. Critics of the church see inculturation initiatives as merely a strategy for conversion and not as a policy of integration with local culture and sentiments. The push for indigenizing Khasi Christians is perceived to be resting on an uneasy foundation from which believers feel pushed to articulate their belonging to the wider social fabric of the clan-based Khasi system while still maintaining their difference as Christians.[33] The Catholic Church has been accused of adopting and upholding traditional dances, songs, and patterns of prayer only for the purpose of pursuing their own syncretic, hidden agenda and not to uphold Khasi culture per se.[34]

The Need for Further Steps Toward Inculturation

The inculturation of the Christian faith among the tribals of Northeast India needs to undergo further steps if the Christian faith is to be part and parcel of the people's worldview and ethos. These steps need to start with a proper understanding of tribal consciousness and the nature of tribal culture. The general conception of tribal consciousness as forming part of the subaltern consciousness of the country – that is, of people who are on the fringe of society socially, economically, culturally, and politically[35] – does not correspond to the perception of tribal peoples in Northeast India, since they understand themselves as simply *jaitbynriew* (people) and inhabitants of their own ancestral land. The term "tribal" is a modern legal category which does not come from within Khasi tradition, and rather than accepting that they exist on the fringe of a general or wider society, they feel that they live right in the centre of the earth in their own homeland, given not by any external worldly authority but by God and their ancestors, with the navel of heaven right in their midst. Further, they do not feel that they live socially, economically, or politically on

32. J. F. Jyrwa, *Christianity in Khasi Culture* (Shillong: Ri Khasi Publications, 2018 [2010]), 5.

33. Paramita Ghosh, 'How Khasi Christians in Meghalaya are Making the Church Their Own', The Hindustan Times https://www.hindustantimes.com/india-news/how-khasi-christians-in-meghalaya-are-making-the-church-their-own/stay-xv1uyk50pdfGbnicMTX790.html

34. Mankular Gashnga, "No place to live and no place to die: the Khasi Niam Tynrai in their own motherland," *The Shillong Times* (19 August 2017).

35. N. Minj, "Meaning of Tribal Consciousness," *Religion and Society* 36, no. 2 (1989): 12.

the fringes of a wider society, but suspect that peoples from elsewhere pose threats to the resources and opportunities available in their land and society.

Again, tribal culture is often described as tending to maintain the status quo; a type of culture in which people rarely critique it and regard change and development as self-destructive rather than formative. In the process of maintaining themselves and preserving their identity, they tend to perpetuate a number of untruths clothed in the guise of laws and principles meant for the common good.[36] In fact in the precolonial and premodern period, Khasi society (and I believe all tribal communities in Northeast India) was never static and rigid, but dynamic and evolving in response to emerging existential requirements. Prior to the advent of modernity, the need to maintain their identity did not arise, since although change might have taken place in their customs, their underlying traditions and identity were always intact. In reality, it was the documentation of prevailing customs in written form that accompanied the advent of colonialism and the onset of modernity which resulted in the freezing of tribal culture in the attempt to defend their own identity against emerging external influences.

A particular human culture, whether tribal or non-tribal, can rarely be said to be good or bad. Only the prevailing customs in the culture may be seen as good or bad, and only with reference to some contexts. Customs are relevant and functional within certain sets of natural and social situations and pass through historical time to grow, reproduce, or die naturally in accordance with the emergent requirements of the society. Customs are transitory and amendable even according to tribal cultural traditions. However, customs do not make instantaneous amendments, as happens in modern legal processes enacted in parliaments, because they are gradually and continuously self-amending according to social changes. The patterns of change and modification of the customs of a particular culture emerge through historical time in response to particular circumstances and constitute the community's traditions. Hence, in spite of changes taking place in their customs, their traditions may still remain.

The evolution of Khasi customs according to living traditions was still in motion when the British, through documentation and administrative actions, declared once and for all time that such and such are the customs of the Khasis. When the dynamic traditions of an oral society are reduced to writing and then become the basis of laws, the natural dynamism of the society is arrested, and the self-amending customs become static, rigid, and as infallible as divine revelations. Thus, customs become greater than traditions, and the elements

36. Fernandez, "Process of Growth," 368.

of a culture which were unjust and appear as untruths are clothed in the guise of laws and principles. Redundant customs which have lost their relevance in the present social situations are codified and used to create legal instruments.

At present, most of the customs documented in academic narratives and legal instruments concerning tribal peoples are no longer relevant and have become dysfunctional and unjust because they have ceased to be relevant or accurate with regard to existing cultural traditions. Hence, there is continual tension between documented customs and the current empirical social situations under which people are living. For example in the premodern period, Khasi custom did not allow women to attend a public *dorbar* on grounds that were justifiable based on the tradition of respect for women. But these grounds are no longer justifiable today, and the custom of barring women from attending public *dorbar* is contradictory to the Khasi tradition of respect for women. Moreover, the Khasi matrilineal clan has lost much of its institutional character. The nuclear family has emerged as the basic unit of society, and the father has taken over the status and role of *kni* (maternal uncle) as the institutional leader. The land is no longer under the control of the people as a community but is owned as private property by powerful and rich individuals, and no longer certified by customs or traditions but by the legal instruments of the modern state. Hence, contemplating inculturation only in terms of age-old customs which are conserved in academic narratives and legal instruments might run contrary to the actual need of the social situations of contemporary people in existing tribal societies.

From the Christian spiritual point of view, it is true that inculturation must begin with people's struggle for justice and the fight against antisocial and oppressive situations in a rapidly changing society. There can also be a tendency to reduce Jesus Christ and Christian mission to a very powerful protest symbol and an instrument merely for creating a just human society with temporal well-being and harmony.[37] According to Pope John Paul in his *Tertio Millennio Adveniente*, N. 38,[38] Christianity cannot compromise the truth that Christ is the one Mediator between God and mankind, and the sole Redeemer of the world, to be clearly distinguished from the founders of other great religions.[39]

37. S. Karotemprel, "The Shape of Christian Mission in the Third Millennium," in *He Taught: A Festschrift in Honour of Sylvanus Sngi Lyngdoh, SDB*, eds. G. Kattuppallil, and Jose Varickkasseril (Shillong: Vendrame Institute Publications, 1996), 306.

38. Pope John Paul II, *Tertio Millennio Adveniente*, N. 38 (1994), https://w2.vatican.va/content/john-paul-ii/en/apost_letters/1994/documents/hf_jp-ii_apl_19941110_tertio-millennio-adveniente.html.

39. See Karotemprel, "Shape of Christian Mission," 307.

"To believe in Jesus," says Albert Nolan, "is to believe that he is divine."[40] So if the church does not preach the "gospel of God . . . regarding his Son . . . who through the Spirit of holiness was appointed the Son of God in power by his resurrection from the dead" (Rom 1:1–4), it has no reason to exist.[41]

The power of the Holy Spirit is universal in time and space and has been among the human race in every culture and community since the beginning of time. What is needed among Christian communities is the manifestation of divine power and authority in the name of Jesus Christ who said, "All authority in heaven and on earth has been given to me" (Matt 28:18). In this age of reason and materialism, even theologians may deny the existence of the spiritual world which tribal peoples still firmly believe to be part of reality. Indeed, we cannot in the religious language of liturgy and theology say that Satan and demons of the Bible are real while in rationalistic and academic contexts we rationalize Satan and the demons and treat them as nothing but the creations of ignorant people's superstitious minds. Even if someone says so with assumed ecclesiastical authority, the simple tribal folks can clearly see through such hypocrisy.

During the days of the missionaries, the people of Raid Nongtluh in Ri Bhoi District of Meghalaya were continually tormented by a demon whom they believed was haunting a rock in the area. It is said that Miss Annie Wozencraft-Thomas of the Welsh Presbyterian Mission prayed fervently for deliverance from such powers, and the demon-haunted rock was struck into pieces by lightning, thereby liberating the Khasi people from their fear. This demonstration of the liberating power of Christ sowed the seed of Christian faith in Ri Bhoi District of Meghalaya. More recently Fr. Sngi Lyngdoh, one of the champions of inculturation in the Khasi and Jaintia Hills, said that he followed the Khasi religious principle of *kit-yyndang bah-ryndang* (readiness to lay down one's neck as a sacrifice). The mortal remains of Joiñ Manik, *Syiem* (chief) of Hima Sohra, had been lying in the house of Drostimai Syiemsad, the niece of the deceased *Syiem*, for twenty-two years, six months, and eleven days since his death on the 11 June 1963. His successor had failed to perform the necessary cremation ceremony, and no one in Hima Sohra, or in the whole of the Khasi and Jaintia Hills, dared to perform the traditional ceremony which might incur deadly consequences since it could be performed only by a male clan member of the deceased *Syiem*, who was also to be his successor. With the

40. A. Nolan, *Jesus Before Christianity* (Mumbai: Society of St Pauls; New York: Orbis, 1976), 198–99.

41. Karotemprel, "Shape of Christian Mission," 308.

consent of Drostimai Syiemsad, Fr. Sngi performed the cremation ceremony on 22 December 1985 on the principle of *kit-ryndang bah-ryndang*, that is, he was ready to bear the consequences of his act. Almost all who witnessed the ceremony were apprehensive; many eagerly expected that he would fall down dead as soon as he touched the preserved bones of the deceased *Syiem*. Drostimai Syiemsad herself was terrified as an abnormal change of weather suddenly took place, and dark, gloomy clouds covered the sky accompanied by thunder and lightning. Fr. Sngi assured her, "Don't be afraid, *ngan kit manga* (I will bear the consequence)," and he proceeded with the ceremony. It is said that Drostimai testified that after the cremation ceremony had been performed, she was liberated from the torments she had suffered for more than twenty-two years. She passed away at the age of ninety-two, that is, eight years after the cremation of the remains of her maternal uncle, and her burial ceremony was performed by Fr. Sngi on the 31 October 1993.[42] Fr. Sngi did not fall down dead. After having lived for ninety-five years, he departed from this world on the 28 May 2016, more than twenty years after he had successfully performed the dreaded cremation ceremony.

It was reported from Brazil that copper miners described how for their own safety they took food and liquor every day to offer in worship to a demon whose figure they had constructed inside the mine to prevent it from collapsing. These simple miners innocently confessed, "Outside we are Catholics, but here inside this mine we worship the demon." This is the same situation Khasi Christians are facing. People need liberation from their troubles, sorrows, and sufferings not only in pepped up and highly emotional healing conventions organized once in a blue moon, but in sober moments in their day-to-day life in their own homes and localities. Church pastors have observed that in cases of sickness where modern medicine and treatment is either unavailable or ineffective, Christians are compelled to seek the service of egg breakers of the Khasi traditional religion since the church has no functional substitute for divination.[43] In fact, Christians choose to consult indigenous shamans and Hindu tantrics in times of trouble rather than turn to their priests and pastors. A majority of the Khasi Christians say, "In the church we worship Jesus Christ along with priests and pastors for the sake of the future life of the soul, but privately at home we have to consult the shamans for the sake of the present earthly life of the body." They justify this dual faith on the basis of

42. R. Kharkrang, *Ka Jingim bad Jinghikai jong u Ph. Sylvanus Sngi Lyngdoh, SDB* (Shillong: Vendrame Institute Publications, 2015), 99–107.

43. Jyrwa, *Christianity in Khasi Culture*, 84.

Jesus' exhortation, "Give back to Caesar what is Caesar's, and to God what is God's" (Matt 22:21).

This belief and attitude of tribal Christians will remain and Christianity will continue to be perceived as a foreign religion as long as the Christian faith is expressed through external cultural forms and scholarly theological semantics. Inculturation needs to take place among tribal peoples in the formation of faith and its dynamic expressions. Tribal people, including the Khasis, have a firm belief and strong faith in the manifested spiritual power of traditional religious rituals because they believe these rituals have effective power to relate to the powerful spiritual world. Can the church now provide for these people a better, superior sense of refuge and security against the material and spiritual forces of nature? If Christianity is to be truly liberative, it must be able to meet these tribal aspirations. Academic theology and rationalistic arguments are of no use in a fight against the power of demons: "Faith by itself, if it is not accompanied by action, is dead" (Jas 2:17). True inculturation among tribal people will happen only when Christianity can demonstrably meet the people's yearning for security and refuge in their existential encounters, materially, socially, and spiritually. If the yearning of the people for physical and spiritual security is adequately met, no matter in what forms of external culture the faith is clothed, it will be in tune with the traditions of the tribal peoples.

8

The Integration of Khasi Traditional Music in the Christian Churches of Shillong, Meghalaya

Donovan K. Swer and Maribon Viray

As a previous chapter shows, the Khasi people in the State of Meghalaya traditionally practiced indigenous forms of worship and faith expressions. Music was integrated within their spiritual world, and they possessed their own form of traditional music related to religious beliefs known as *Ka Niam Khasi* (Khasi religion). Using the traditional instruments described in this chapter, music accompanied prayer, chanting, sacrifices, dances, and festivals. With the introduction of Christianity and the growth of churches in the Khasi Hills, including among others Catholics, Presbyterians, Baptists, and the Church of North India, converted Khasis slowly moved away from traditional music due to its perceived link with "animism" or pagan practices. Moreover, differences in the styles of music and the expression of worship can be observed between the Christian denominations. The current scenario in church music is changing as some aspects of traditional music are being recovered and incorporated within Christian worship. The factors which have led to these observed changes are discussed in this chapter.[1] We ask to what extent the integration of traditional

1. See Gosh, P., *How Khasi Christians in Meghalaya are Making the Church Their Own Hindustan Times* (February 6, 2027). https://hindustantimes.com/india-news/how-khasi-christians-in-meghalaya-are-making-the-church-their-own/story-xvluyk50pfGbnlcMTxM790.html

Figure 1: Source-Field Work 2017
Shad Suk Mynsiem

music is impacting the church today, and specifically, how it is perceived by young worship leaders.

Introduction of Christianity among the Khasis

The origins of Protestant missions among the Khasi people can be traced to the decision of the Welsh Calvinistic Methodists to sever their connection with the London Missionary Society in order to form their own distinctive organization promoting missionary work. This new society sent a thirty-year-old man named Thomas Jones, together with his new bride Ann, to commence work in Northeast India in 1840. Jones was a remarkable man whose approach to missionary work reflected his working class, Welsh background, but his labours in the Jaintia Hills ultimately resulted in tragedy when he was dismissed from the mission because of his active promotion of Khasi converts' economic and material well-being. This activity was regarded by the Welsh mission committee in Britain as being "to the detriment . . . of the struggle for Khasi souls." Thomas Jones remained in the Jaintia Hills as an independent missionary, but he later clashed with imperialist business people whose greed and injustice he openly challenged. He was driven out of the region and died a broken man in Calcutta in 1849. Jones' grave, long abandoned and forgotten, was rediscovered by David Syiemlieh in 1986 and became a site of pilgrimage for Khasi Christians wishing to honour: the memory of the man known to many as "the founding father of the Khasi alphabet and literature."[2]

Khasi scholars have commented on the similarities between their traditional culture and that of the early Welsh missionaries. Wales is a mountainous country, and its people possessed their own language and traditions, including a particular type of music. Often called "the land of song," the Welsh valleys rang with hymn singing of a distinctive kind, leading one Khasi commentator to speak of the "remarkable similarity" between the Welsh and Khasi people. In addition, Welsh Christianity in the nineteenth and early twentieth centuries was profoundly influenced by movements of spiritual revival in which the reality of invisible, spiritual powers was recognized and the work of the Holy Spirit had a significance which was not often found in other forms of Western Christianity.

Nonetheless, from the beginning Christian missionaries met with strong opposition from the practitioners of traditional religion. The first conversions resulted in considerable unrest, and there were attempts to abduct the converts from the mission compounds in which they were confined. In 1899, a movement known as *Seng Khasi* was begun to "foster a sense of brotherhood amongst the Khasi who still retain their socio-cultural and religious heritage." The Welsh historian Nigel Jenkins wrote in 1993 of "the harm done to the Christian cause by the missionaries' virtual demonization of the indigenous culture, to the exclusion of Khasi thought-forms and musical traditions." He added that while the churches of Mizoram "throb with the rhythms of native drums," the *duitara* (Figure 2) and the *tangmuri* (Figure 3) were "virtual strangers to the churches of the Khasi."[3]

2. The source for this information is an unpublished article: Nigel Jenkins, "Thomas Jones and the Church He Founded in the Khasi Jaintia Hills," a paper presented at Souvenir: Church History Association Triennial Conference, Shillong in 1993. A photocopy of the paper was given to David Smith by a Catholic Nun from Northeast India during a conference at the Overseas Mission Studies Centre in New Haven, USA, a meeting which providentially triggered his growing awareness of the significance of the Christian presence in this region. The connection between Welsh Methodists and the Khasi people was very strong in the early twentieth century, as can be seen in publications in the Welsh language which reported on the growth of the church in NE India. Additional sources related to this story are 'How a historian stumbled upon the tomb of Thomas Jones', *Shillong Times,* June 24, 2019. https://theshillongtimes.com/2019/06/24/how-a-historian-stumbled-upon-tomb-of-thomas-jones/ and 'A History of Khasi Language and Literature', Central Institute of Indian Language. http://lisindia.ciil.org/Khasi/Khasi_Hist.html#:~:text=Thomas%20Jones%20one%20become%20known,literacy%2C%education%20and%Khasi%20writings

3. Jenkins, *Gwalia in Khasia* (Llandysul: Gomer Press, 1995).

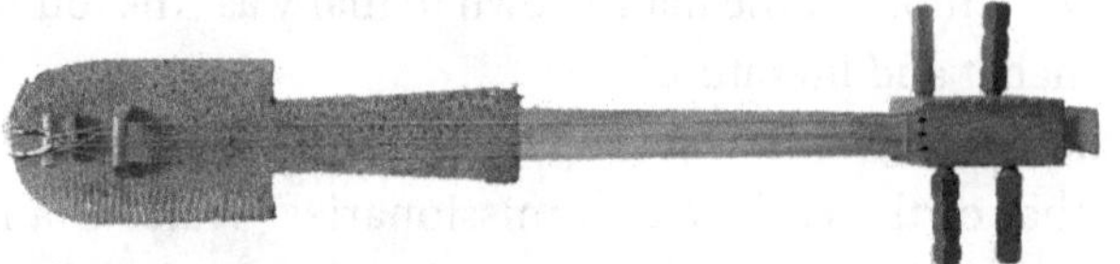

Figure 2: ***Source: Field Work 2018***

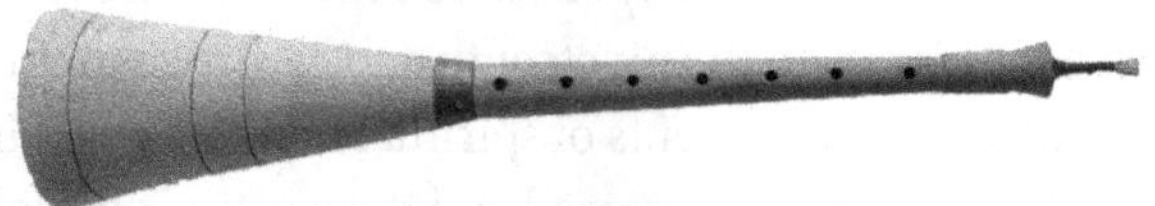

Figure 3: ***Source: Field Work 2018***

Table 1: Percentage of Religion in Meghalaya[4]

Religion	Percentage
Christian	70.25%
Other Indigenous religions	5.25%
Hinduism	13.27%
Muslim/Islam	3.27%
Sikhism, Jainism, Buddhism	2.71%

At present Christians constitute 70.3 percent of the population of the State of Meghalaya according to census findings in 2011. Not only did Christian missionaries bring Western modes of worship and music to the Northeast of India, but with the arrival of Roman Catholics in the form of Salvatorian missionaries from Germany in 1890, a radically different form of Western music was introduced to the tribal peoples. In contrast to Welsh hymn singing, the Catholics brought their own Latin hymnody, or Gregorian chant, singing sacred Latin texts without instrumental accompaniment. The arrival of yet other denominations in the course of time only increased the complexity and variety of worship patterns in the growing churches among the Khasi. By the 1960s, there was increasing demand for contextualization as many people asked, "Where is the Khasiness in your worship and theology?" J. Fortis Jyrwa comments that had missionaries and their early converts taken seriously the

4. State, M., & Part, R. (2018). Meghalaya State Rural Part Religion wise distribution of population, 1–10

need to use and enrich Khasi traditional and cultural forms, the history of evangelization in Meghalaya would have looked very different because "genuine evangelization means indigenisation."[5] It is precisely this challenge which is now being faced and is the motivation behind this research.

Western hymns were translated into the Khasi language, a hymn book was gradually prepared, and church choirs were formed. Eventually, these translations led to the composition of original hymns and songs. These local compositions were accepted and became an integral part of church worship, together with their accompanying tunes which reflected indigenous musical elements, including drum beats and tonal characteristics derived from Khasi tradition. For example, traditional music includes a distinctive style of singing in which a note is sung with a slur and sustained with a particular tonal effect and distinctive form of pronunciation of the lyrics. This way of singing in the Khasi dialect clearly creates a feeling of pride and ownership and might be described as a type of informal contextualization.

We reproduce here two examples of songs which are sung to the accompaniment of the traditional drumbeat *Ka Ksing Shadwait* (*Ksing* means drum; *shad* means dance; *wait* means sword).[6] The first is from the *Church of God Meghalaya and Assam Hymn Book*, and the second comes from the *Khasia-Jaintia Hymn Book*:

5. J. Fortis Jywra, "The Missionaries and the Khasi Jaintia People." This lecture also included in the information provided as described above. It was published in *New Welsh Review* Cardiff, 1993 and originally delivered at the Church History Association of India Triennial Conference in Shillong in 1993. The same author published *Christianity in Khasi Culture* (Shillong: Rikhaji Publishers, 2018).

6. L. Syiem, *The Evolution of Khasi Music: A Study of the Classical Content* (New Delhi: Regency, 2005).

Kyrhai ka jingngeit, kyrkhai ka jingisynei
Kyrhai ka jingim ngi la ioh mynta
Kyrhai ka jingsuk, kyrhai ka jingkmen
Kyrkhai U Jisu u la ia nga[7]

Free translation

Abundant faith, abundant mercy
Abundant life we receive right now
Abundant peace, abundant joy
Abundantly Jesus gave to me

Ngin jop da ka t jingngeit
Ngin jop da ka j jingngeit
Oh da jingjop don Burom burom
Ngin jo pia ka pyrthei[8]

Free translation

We will win by faith
We will win by faith
With glorious victory
We will win the world

7. *Ki Jingrwai Shem Mynsiem* (Inspired Hymns), Church of God Hymnal book, 16th edition, Shillong,2001.

8. *Ka Kot Jingrwai ban mane ia U Blei ha ka ri Khasi bad Jaiñtia* (A Hymnal book to worship God in Khasi and Jaiñtia Hills), published by the Synod Khasi Jaiñtia Presbyterian Church, Shillong, 2002

***KaKsing Shadwait* drumbeat:** *Tem beit* (Variation1)[9]

Ksing Shadwait
Tem beit (Variation 1)
♩=120
Ksing Shynrang (Male drum)
Nakra (Big drum)
Kynshaw (Small Cymbals)

Traditional Music and Instruments

This chapter is the fruit of our research into the status and use of Khasi traditional music, both the instruments belonging to that tradition and the rhythms and structures of the music itself, in Christian churches in the city of Shillong, the capital of the State of Meghalaya. This location is significant since Khasi Christians in this context confront the pressures of an urban culture in which the forces of modernization and development are especially strong. Young people in particular are exposed to the influences of what has been called an international youth culture which includes modern, Western forms of music that are far removed from the world of Khasi traditions. Since young people often play important roles in leading worship, this research aimed to discover their attitudes toward traditional music and to gauge the extent to which it is being rediscovered and used for the worship of God by churches in Shillong today.

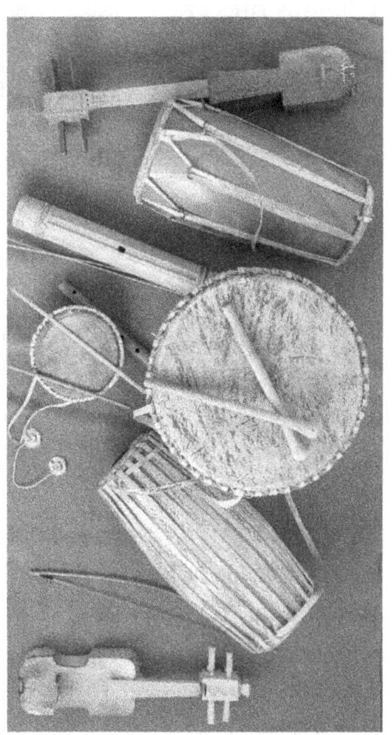

Figure 4: ***Source: Field Work 2021***
Khasi Traditional Musical Instrument

It has been said that Western musical instruments are socially acceptable in a manner that traditional ones are not, so that a musician playing a guitar will attract

9. Also taken from L. Syiem, *The Evolution of Khasi Music*. (Adapted to staff notation by chapter author.)

praise in a way that is unlikely to be given to someone skilful in the playing a traditional instrument, even though the latter may require considerable dedication and skill.[10] Respondents for this study were drawn from churches belonging to six different denominations, and all respondents were actively engaged in church music, whether as choir directors, praise leaders, solo singers, or musicians involved in other genres of Christian music. All participants had been engaged in church music for a minimum of ten years, and all took part in focus group discussions of the issues raised in this chapter.

In a book entitled *The Evolution of Khasi Traditional Music: A Study of the Classical Content*, Dr. L. Syiem notes that this music involves both complex structures and a wide range of instruments. She identifies no less than *shiphew ksing bad arphew hymnniew* skit (ten units of drums and twenty-seven drumbeats).[11] Religious drumbeats are used only for performing explicitly religious rites and rituals, whereas others are used on social occasions such as festivals and celebrations. Among the latter are *Ka Ksing Shadwait* (a sword dance beat), *Ka Ksing Lumpaid* (a drumbeat to assemble or gather people), and *Ka Ksing Mastieh* (a drumbeat to come with joy and rejoice). The taxonomy of traditional instruments includes a wide variety in addition to the drums already mentioned including string, wind, and reed instruments.

As we have seen, traditional music – whether the music itself or the purpose for which it was used, and even the actual instruments – was treated with suspicion by missionaries and their early converts since it was claimed that this music was associated with "animism" and "pagan practice." Nigel Jenkins notes the dismissive reaction of one missionary who described Khasi singing and chanting as "like screaming" and said that they "had no music of their own."[12] Another missionary encountered Khasi Christians celebrating a harvest in traditional style and described the scene as follows: "When they saw me coming near, half the noise ceased. Having glanced around I asked the man of the house what the great commotion meant? He answered that it was their rice feast. I asked was this kind of thing worthy and seemly for a Christian to observe?"[13]

Not surprisingly, attitudes like these toward traditional music, especially when these attitudes were backed up by the threat of suspension or even

10. Based on focus group discussion with church leaders, Shillong, 3 April 2019.

11. Syiem, *Evolution of Khasi Music*.

12. Jenkins, *Gwalia in Khasia*, 289.

13. John Hughes Morris, *The History of the Welsh Calvinistic Methodist Foreign Mission* (New Delhi: Gidwani Indus, 1996 [1910]), 166.

excommunication from the church, resulted in the alienation of early converts from their own cultural heritage. This approach was passed on to following generations and has been reflected in the fundamental patterns of public worship in the churches of Shillong. As a result, Khasi traditional music came to be a sign of identity, whether it was renounced and shunned by Christians or affirmed and celebrated by the defenders of tradition.

Figure 5: ***Source: Field Work 2017***
Shad Suk Mynsiem

We can identify three factors which create difficulties for church musicians and worship leaders who might wish to recover and integrate traditional forms of music into contemporary Christian worship among the Khasi people. First, traditional music was obviously related to the pre-Christian worldview of the people and in both its form and performance reflects that context. This connection includes the consecration of musical instruments by means of a specific ritual which involves calling upon the spirits of the ancestors and dedicating the instruments for sacred purposes. From that point on the instrument becomes a consecrated object which can never be traded in an open market because the owner and musician now have a spiritual attachment to the instrument. This means that for Khasi Christians, traditional instruments seemed to have an organic connection to the traditional worldview and for that reason are regarded as inappropriate for the worship of Christ. However, these fears have diminished in recent times, as traditional instruments are now being made by Christian craftsmen and dedicated to the glory of God. In the past divination was used at every stage in the production process of instrument-making; when the wood was cut, the lace was tied, and so on, permission and help were sought through prayer and ritual to ensure that good sounds would come from the instrument.[14] Christian craftsmen are now replacing this traditional divination process with a contextualized act of consecration, leading one respondent to say, "the instruments are not evil."

Second are specifically musical challenges; the range and versatility of music may be limited by the nature of traditional instruments. For example, the Khasi stringed instrument called *ka duitara* (Figure 2) can be tuned only in a single key, so changing the key of a song is difficult. However, these kinds of difficulties have occurred frequently in the history of all musical traditions and have been overcome by the evolution of new musical forms and instruments. New developments do not invalidate the previous styles on which they depended, and traditional Khasi music is likely to show the same adaptability.

A third challenge relates to something mentioned earlier in this chapter, namely what has often been called the generation gap. In the context of the urban culture of a city like Shillong, young people are influenced by modernist cultural forces which may result in their perception that traditional music belongs to the older generation and is unable to connect with the realities they face in contemporary society. Furthermore, since worship leaders in most churches are often young people, they may be inclined to privilege contemporary forms of music often described as "praise and worship." This phrase relates to contemporary songs that use repetition of phrases and verses and are accompanied by bands playing guitars, pianos or keyboards, and drums. Some praise leaders have integrated Khasi language and instruments in their sung worship, but more often the trend is toward Western styles of music replacing traditional practice.

However, it is interesting to note that worship music has recently included a feature called "spontaneous worship," the creation of a new song within the actual context of the worship service. This worship is not pre-planned nor practiced in advance but comes into being during the time of worship. What is fascinating is that this practice recalls an aspect of Khasi traditional music called *phawar* in which new songs are created during traditional worship and celebrations. Something now being hailed as a new development in spontaneity in urban worship turns out to have a precedent in the practice of *phawar* which existed among the Khasi people for ages past.[15]

14. Syiem, *Evolution of Khasi Music*, 79.

15. Focus group discussion with church leaders, Shillong, 3 April 2019.

Khasi Traditional Music: Present and Future

The Khasi people possess an indigenous style of music and singing which, despite the attempted suppression of traditional music in the course of Christian evangelization, has remained and can be detected even during the use of hymns which originated in Europe. When such hymns are sung in a free rhythm and without instrumental accompaniment, the underlying patterns of traditional music become evident. However, at present there are indications of the renewal of traditional music, notwithstanding the various difficulties and challenges to it discussed in this chapter. We conclude by noticing three factors which are contributing to the recovery of Khasi traditions specifically in the context of Christian worship.

First, in Khasi tradition music and dance are very closely related, and the revival of cultural dancing has at the same time aroused renewed interest in Khasi music. Various celebrations and festivals throughout each year are marked by music and dance for which traditional dress is worn and the drums beaten. This revival of culture has been embraced by many churches, often in specifically organized programmes designed to inculcate these indigenous practices.[16]

Second in the sphere of education, music schools now play a vital role as training centres encouraging the development of skills in vocal and instrumental music, creating space and providing tools for students to explore aspects of music. This exploration includes Khasi traditional music which was once transmitted by oral tradition, but now the music schools provide accessibility for all to learn and understand, opening the door for everyone to enjoy playing musical instruments. Some churches have initiatives to set up music education and to teach individuals the skills of traditional music. Khasi folk musicians from the schools have had a huge impact and contributed to the growth of interest in traditional music.

Third, we mentioned earlier the shifting patterns of congregational singing in the churches of Shillong, but another common feature of worship is of special importance to this subject: namely the role of choirs in Khasi Christian worship. Choirs are an important aspect of church life and play a major role in regular worship services. Choral music includes songs in four-part harmony, but this is not a rigid practice, and there has been a massive integration of Khasi traditional music within the repertoires of church choirs. The Khasi drumbeats discussed earlier are allowed to accompany choirs and have become the cornerstone of many choral performances in Shillong and

16. Focus group discussion with church leaders, Shillong, 3 April 2019.

wider afield. These drumbeats, once rejected as alien to Christianity, have been used along with the range of traditional string, percussion, and reed instruments to accompany church choral music and glorify Jesus Christ in the city of Shillong. Khasi traditional dress for men and women is worn so that choral performance has played a major role in the integration of traditional music into the Christian churches of Shillong.

Finally, we must note that apart from the regular week-by-week worship of individual congregations, there are every year a series of large gatherings of Christians during which traditional music is performed without objections from pastors or church leaders. This lack of objections suggests acceptance of Khasi culture and traditional music as a means to glorify God, and it may also be evidence of a reappraisal of the relationship between the gospel and tribal cultures. The attitudes of individual congregations can still vary a great deal, but a general trend can be discerned that the musical heritage of the Khasi people may make a contribution to the "new song" of the redeemed.

Conclusion

One of our respondents observed that churches in Shillong initially resisted the use of guitars in Christian worship since the guitar was deemed to be a secular

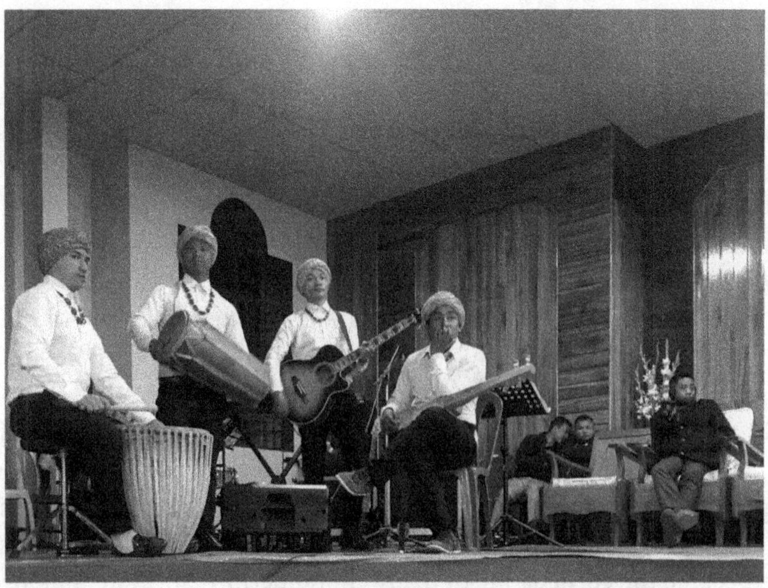

Figure 6: ***Church Service 2019***

instrument associated with rock music and a view of life which was contrary to the gospel. Yet over time the guitar not only became accepted but actually came to dominate Christian music in the region. The situation with Khasi musical instruments is similar, yet different. They too have been suspect and regarded as unsuitable for church worship. Yet in this case the objection was not because they are associated with a secular worldview, but with a sacred one. If then guitars, despite their secular use in popular culture, could be sanctified and contribute to the praise of Christ, how much more naturally might Khasi instruments with a tradition of consecration and spirituality be "converted" and used in the praise of the God and Father of Jesus Christ. At this time the use of traditional music for the expression of the Christian faith is minimal, and in some churches it is on the verge of social and cultural extinction. Church leaders are the key agents to promote the integration of Khasi music within church worship and to overcome the pagan and evil connotations which continue to shape congregational attitudes on this subject. The Khasi Christian churches have been deeply influenced by Western culture, including with regard to music and musical instruments; there is an urgent need for them to appropriate their own cultural resources for the glory of God. This study has identified an emerging trend in which Khasi traditional musicians are being recognized as possessing gifts and skills capable of enriching Christian worship, and it is hoped this trend will expand until, like the crowd on the day of Pentecost, the Khasi will ask concerning traditional music: "How is it that each of us hears in our own native language?" (see Acts 2:6).

9

Myth in Kuki Tradition – The Search for Meaning

Fr. Peter Haokip

My understanding of and appreciation for tribal myths began with my study of the Bible, especially with access to the monumental collection of numerous ancient myths by scholars responsible for the volume *Ancient Near Eastern Texts Relating to the Old Testament*.[1] I also came across the American author Joseph Campbell, a leading exponent of myth.[2] He is described by reviewers of his books as "the rarest of intellectuals in American life: a serious thinker, who has been embraced by the popular culture".[3] Campbell has written numerous books on the mythology of the East and West. I also came to know about the works of Harry Verrier Elwin (1902–1964), the Anglican priest-missionary who came to India in 1927 and spent twenty-one years of his life among the tribal peoples of Central India (1932–1953). In 1953, Jawharlal Nehru, the first Prime Minister of India, appointed Verrier Elwin as an advisor on tribal affairs to the government of India and he spent eleven years with the tribals in North East India until his death in 1964. Elwin wrote much about the myths of the tribal peoples, and Nari Rustomji, the predecessor of Elwin as

1. James B. Pritchard, ed., *Ancient Near Eastern Texts Relating to the Old Testament*, 3rd ed. (Princeton: Princeton University Press, 1982). This monumental collection contains texts of all the ancient Near Eastern peoples and is a sine qua non for biblical scholars.

2. Joseph Campbell's books include *The Hero with a Thousand Faces* (Princeton: Princeton University Press, 1973) and a series under the title *The Masks of God* covering oriental, occidental, and other mythologies (New York: Doubleday Anchor Books, 1959–1987).

3. Joseph Campbell with Bill Moyers, *The Power of Myth* (New York: Doubleday, 1988), back cover commendations.

advisor on tribal affairs provided in his book *Verrier Elwin - Philanthropologist: Selected Writings* a detailed list of Elwin's the books and articles.[4] Rustomji called Verrier Elwin a "philanthropologist" because, as Elwin himself said,

> The essence and art of anthropology is love. Without it nothing is fertile, nothing is true. For me anthropology did not mean "field work" it meant my whole life. My method was to settle down among the people, live with them, share their life as far as an outsider could.[5]

In a bibliography section of nine pages are about 160 references to studies related to tribals and their cultures between 1934 and Elwin's death in 1964, ranging from books to articles in newspapers, journals, radio talks, etc.[6] His nineteen books on tribes would alone make Elwin one of the outstanding experts on the cultures and myths of the tribes of India. So large was his contribution to the study of tribal culture that it must make him unmatched by anyone else; he painstakingly collected and documented tribal myths, stories, and folksongs in works such as *Myths and Dreams of the Baigas of Middle India* (1937), *The Folk Tales of Mahakoshal* (1944), *Myths of Middle India* (1949), *Tribal Myths of Orissa* (1954), *Myths of the North East Frontier of India* (1968), and *A New Book of Tribal Fiction* (1976).

Another author whose work has been significant is Carlos Maesters, a Brazilian biblical scholar and expert on the myths of native South American Indian tribes. I also came to know a number of authors, including some Europeans, whose interest in mythology is reflected in their widely read works of fantasy including J. J. R. Tolkien, author of *The Lord of the Rings* and *The Hobbit*. The second writer, who was a close friend of Tolkien, is C. S. Lewis, the author of *The Chronicles of Narnia* and *The Screwtape Letters*. In addition, I have learned from the author Amish Tripati whose Shiva trilogy, *The Immortals of Meluha, The Secrets of the Nagas,* and *The Oath of the Vayuputras*has turned Indian myths into bestselling reads today.[7]

---

4. Verrier Elwin and Nari Rustomji, *Verrier Elwin Philanthropologist: Selected Writings* (Delhi: North-Eastern Hill University Publications, 1989)

5. Verrier Elwin, *The Tribal World of Verrier Elwin: An Autobiography* (Oxford: Oxford University Press, 1964), 142. Elwin was not an anthropologist by training. He obtained a double first-class degree in classics and theology but was conferred a doctorate in anthropology by the University of Oxford for his contribution anthropolological studies.

6. Verrier and Rustomji, *Verrier Elwin Philanthropologist*, 371–79

7. Amish Tripati, *The Immortals of Meluha* (New Delhi: Westland, 2010); *The Secrets of the Nagas* (New Delhi: Westland, 2011); and *The Oath of the Vayuputras* (New Delhi: Westland, 2013).

What Is Myth?

The New Oxford Dictionary of English defines myth first as "a traditional story, especially one concerning the early history of a people or explaining some natural or social phenomenon, typically involving supernatural beings or events," and second as "a widely held but false belief or idea."[8] In popular daily parlance, myth is understood in the second way. However, social scientists and others are increasingly aware of the importance and significance of myths especially among tribal or indigenous peoples around the world. Myths can be said to possess "an intensity of meaning that is akin to poetry."[9] According to Joseph Campbell, even if myths are ignored they will catch us because myths are clues to the spiritual potentialities of human life. He describes myths as teaching that "you can turn inward and you begin to get the message of the symbols."

> Read other people's myths, not those of your own, because you tend to interpret your own religion in terms of facts – but if you read the others' ones, you will begin to get the message. Myth helps you to put your mind in touch with this experience of being alive. It tells you what the experience is. Marriage, for example! What is marriage? The myth tells you what it is. It's the reunion of the separated dyad. Originally you were one. You are now two in the world, but the recognition of the spiritual identity is what marriage is.[10]

Campbell quotes Rollo May as saying that "there is so much violence in American society today because there are no more great myths to help young men and women to relate to the world or to understand that world beyond what is seen."[11] The same could be true of the societies of the Northeast of India. Campbell taught mythology for thirty-eight years, and when asked about the response of youth to myths, he said, "Young people just grab this stuff. Mythology teaches you what is behind literature and the arts, it teaches you about your own life. It's a great, exciting, life nourishing subject."[12] He also said that myths are "stories about the wisdom of life, they really are. What we're

---

8. Judy Pearsall, ed., *The New Oxford Dictionary of English* (Oxford: Clarendon, 1998), 1225.

9. Arthur Cotterell, *A Dictionary of World Mythology* (Oxford: Oxford University Press, 1986), 1.

10. Joseph Campbell, *The Power of Myth* (New York: Anchor/Doubleday,1988), 5.

11. Rollo May quoted in Campbell, *Power of Myth*, 9–10.

12. Campbell, 14.

learning in our schools is not the wisdom of life. We're learning technologies, we're getting information."[13] The myths of the world are, according to Campbell, "the world's dreams. They are archetypal dreams and deal with great human problems."[14]

Verrier Elwin understood the importance of these folklores for the preservation of the identity, values, and ethos of tribal life. He describes his life with the tribal peoples as follows:

> To be among the Baigas was like living in the middle of a fairy story. Of all the tribes I know they are the most possessed by their mythology. And these myths were not just interesting tales tacked on to the fringe of their life. They were alive; every one of them was continually being put into action. When the Baiga was summoned to control a man-eating tiger, he faced this dangerous task with the more courage because he knew that the duty had been his from the beginning. When he performed magic on behalf of the Gond farmers, he recited the myth of creation of the world and reminded his hearers of the unique share his tribe had in it. The myth breathed life into ancient custom; it made the intelligible real; it turned the ancient heroes into contemporaries.[15]

In his introduction to *Myths of Middle India*,[16] Elwin has the following to say about myths in general and tribal myths in particular:

> Myth is not a relic of the past, but is a living reality and to some extent controlling the present. Myth as it exists in a tribal community, that is, in its primitive form, is not merely a story told but a reality lived. It is not of the nature of fiction, such as we read today in a novel, but it is a living reality, believed to have once happened in primeval times, and continuing ever since to influence the world and human destinies. This myth is to the savage what to the fully believing Christian, is the Biblical story of Creation, of the Fall, of the Redemption.[17]

---

13. Campbell, 11.

14. Campbell, 19–20.

15. Elwin, *Tribal World*, 146.

16. Verrier Elwin, *Myths of Middle India* (Delhi: Vanya Prakashan; Oxford: Oxford University Press, 1991, [1949]).

17. Elwin, *Myths of Middle India*, xiv. Elwin's discussion of myths reveals his deep respect for tribal cultures, so that his use of terms like "savage" does not indicate racial or cultural prejudice, but reflects theories of religious history and development current at that time.

According to Carlos Maesters, a Brazilian biblical scholar who writes about the cultures of South American native Indian tribes,

> Myth is like a catalyst in the tribe's life. It is the key the Indian holds to read and interpret all that exists and all that happens. Their myth is the tribe's encyclopaedia. Everything is in it. The myth is the tribe's tradition, its rule of life, its law, its medicine, its past, its present and its future. Whatever is important for the life of the tribe is found in it. You could call the myth the Indians' Bible. It is the expression of their way of life, nature and the world, the consciousness the tribe has of itself as a tribe.[18]

Speaking specifically in the context of Christian evangelization in which the tribal myth has often been discarded, he says,

> Obliterating myths means doing violence to what Indians possess as most truly their own. It is equivalent to tampering with someone's personality. To destroy the personality of another by violence or brain-washing is anti-human and anti-gospel. In the same way, to destroy a people's myth by an approach to evangelization which does not respect the tribe's "difference" and its personality is also anti-human and anti-gospel, because the receptacle that was to contain the gospel message is destroyed, the basic foundation for evangelization and on-going Christian instruction is no longer there.[19]

Evangelization resulting in a people's exile from their identity is, according to Maesters, contrary to the pedagogy of God with the twelve tribes of Israel. It is also contrary to what the church has always preached, namely, "grace builds on nature. Grace does not destroy persons; less still can it destroy a whole tribe."[20] We can also say that the cultural personalities of some of our communities in Northeast India might have been obliterated in the name of evangelization because violence was committed against our cultural identity and personality. Such an approach resulted in some tribes losing their identity and having their very existence as a people threatened.

---

18. Carlos Maesters, "Indian Myths and the Old Testament," *SEDOS Bulletin* 24, no. 3 (1992): 67–73, 69.

19. Carlos Maesters, "Indian Myths and the Two Testaments," *SEDOS Bulletin* 24, no. 8 (1992): 222.

20. Maesters, "Indian Myths," 227–28.

Myths in Kuki Tradition

The word for "myth" and "story" in the Kuki language is the same. The term is *thusim* (history or story). One can distinguish myth from history by describing the former as *malai thuism* or *ton lai thuism* (stories of old). Maybe because of this, it is not easy to distinguish between the end of the mythical period and the beginning of the historical age in Kuki tradition. What is important is that, like the myths referred to above, Kuki myths are identity markers signifying who the people are, their aspirations and hopes, their view of life and the world, and their relationships with all these.

The myth of the origin of the Kuki-Chin-Mizo tribes describes how they came out of a cave in the earth, *khula pen* (literally birth in a cave). This myth is something that unites them and gives them identity. The Kuki myth of Galngam, a heroic figure who embodies strength, bravery, chivalry, and every aspect of character admired in the community, is a favourite myth within this community. Galngam is indeed a Kuki "Superman" whose many exploits and deeds of bravery have been related orally but are yet to be recorded in writing. Another popular mythical figure is Benglam,[21] someone who often appeared and acted very wisely and cunningly. He could be foolish, naive, childlike, and simple and can be identified as a kind of wisdom figure similar to such characters in the Wisdom literature in the Bible in books like Proverbs, Ecclesiastes and the Wisdom of Solomon. There are many episodes of Benglam's exploits as a foolish person as well as someone capable of cunning and wisdom.[22] Two episodes illustrate the contrasting aspects of this character:

> Once upon a time Benglam was returning to his hut in the *jhum* field, and his enemies were waiting for him inside the hut. Sensing the presence of some people in the hut he called out "O Ka Buh"– "Hello my hut." There was silence. He said, "How come, my hut is not responding to me today. Perhaps it is afraid to answer me because some people are there." Now, thinking that the hut used to respond to Benglam, his enemies decided to respond to him if he called again. So when Benglam called out again, "O my hut!" the enemies responded "Ku!" Thus, Benglam confirmed the presence of his enemies and ran away.[23]

---

21. The same folk character is known by different names among the other Kuki tribes.

22. As this mythical character is found among many tribes, research needs to be done to collect and document all the possible episodes of this character.

23. James V. Haokip, *Benglam Thusim –A Thadou-Kuki Trickster of Yore* (Presented at a Symposium at Centre for Creative and Culture Studies, North Eastern Hill University, 2013), 1.

> Once upon a time Benglam went to a far off village and managed to return with a bag of salt. When approaching his village, he was thinking of how to hide that precious bag of salt as it was a rare commodity in his village. He tried many places but thought they were not safe enough. So, at last he hid it under water and placed a big stone over it. When he went with his wife to find it nothing was left as it had dissolved in water.[24]

One of the most touching Kuki myths is *Khupting le Ngambom*.[25] A short version of the myth is as follows:

> Once upon a time there were two women. Both of them were pregnant. They were very friendly to each other, too. Whenever they had a pain in the stomach, they used to make their stomachs touch each other, and their pains would disappear immediately. So they said, "After giving birth, if our children are boys or girls, let us make them *kijol* (friendship between people who have the same name), but if one is a boy and the other a girl, let us make them marry."
>
> When the children were born, one of them was a girl, and she was named Khupting. The other was a boy, and the name Ngambom was given to him. Even when they were little children, they were always together, and when they grew up, they fell in love and wanted to marry. But Khupting's family was against the marriage because while they were still sucklings and were in different cradles, Ngambom used to be seen crawling up to Khupting in the form of *tangnam* (lizard) to be by her side.
>
> Now, once while Ngambom was on a journey, Khupting fell ill and died. As her body was prepared for burial, it grew and grew and could not be taken out through the door. Ngambom then played *gosem* (musical instrument) bidding farewell to her. Only then did the body decrease and could be taken out. But the same thing happened again at the graveyard. Khupting's body grew so big again that the grave could not contain it. Once again, Ngambom had to play the *gosem* to lure her to go.

24. Haokip, *Benglam*, 3.

25. The Meitei tradition has the Khamba and Thoibi epic of love which is well-documented, unlike the Kuki version.

After the burial, a beautiful flower plant (*joujam*) sprang up on the grave, but the flowers were always plucked away, though nobody was seen doing it. One day Ngambom decided to watch over it, and as he was watching a *sajo* (wild cat-like animal), probably the *binturong*[26] came there. Ngambom then asked him, who was the one that sent him, and the animal said his mistress, Khupting, had sent him. "Can I come along with you?" asked Ngambom.

"If you want to come," replied the *sajo*, "then hang on to my tail."

After passing through many dangerous cliffs and precipices, they reached heaven (*van*). But in heaven, the dead people were alive like human beings but only during the day. At night they were just heaps of bones. So Ngambom and Khupting could not really be united. So Khupting said to Ngambom, "If you really want to stay united with me, you have to die first. For this go back to the earth and perform *kilhalhona*[27] with a pig." Accordingly Ngambom went back to the earth carried by a *lailen* (a bird). As he came home, he asked *kilhalhona* to be performed on him. He was lying down while others were busy preparing the meat, and portions of the meat were kept to dry over the hearth, pierced through with iron bars. One of these iron bars fell on him, pierced his chest, and killed him. Thus he was able to be united again with his beloved, Khupting. The picture seen on the moon is of a tree called *Thing-jabong*. In the field of Khupting's family, the branch that is cut off is the one done by Ngambom.[28]

The love of Khupting and Ngambom for each other is immortalized by the picture on the moon, so that every time we see the moon, it reminds us of their love. Another epic story revolves around another beautiful girl, Lenchonghoi. A *lhomi* (lion-man) falls in love with her, and disguised as a handsome boy,

26. A *binturong* is a tree-dwelling Asian civet with a coarse, blackish coat and a muscular prehensile tail. The civet is a slender, nocturnal, carnivorous mammal with a barred and spotted coat and well-developed anal scent glands. Civet cat is an American commercial term for the fur of the ring-tailed cat.

27. *Kilhalhona* literally means to prevent the soul from departing. It is a ritual of well-being with the sacrifice of an animal. A cock or a hen could also be sacrificed for the ceremony.

28. This story has many versions. The version here is recorded from the late Ngamkholet Haokip, my cousin of Imphal, in 1978. This story is considered to be a story of love par excellence, a paragon of love stories.

he elopes with Lenchonghoi. As soon they come to know about the kidnap of their sister, her seven brothers vow to bring their beloved sister back whatever the cost.

The Search for Meaning in Myths

I have referred to Joseph Campbell's warning regarding the tendency to read our own myths as facts. If we cannot read myths as facts, how should we read and interpret them? Ancient peoples were taught truths about life in stories. Even today stories are the most popular ways of teaching people the truths about life and the afterlife, or about God and human beings and their relationships. Perhaps these ancient stories were rooted in some actual realities like love, bravery, and chivalry and the people's hopes and aspirations. One important thing to remember is that we should know the full narrative of the story in order to be able to interpret it properly and identify the message or messages. Truncated versions or summaries of these myths will not enable us to find their proper meanings and significance.

For example, the myth of the origin of the Kuki-Chin-Mizo group of tribes as *Khul a pen* (literally birth from the cave) is obviously not to be understood as like the birth of babies from a mother's womb since these original people were already living a kind of settled life in the underworld. They already celebrated festivals and did other activities like hunting for their food. In fact it was the hunters who discovered an outlet of the cave through which they emerged into the upper world. In this sense, the myth is probably telling us of the emergence of the tribe/tribes from one stage of life to another. Another function of the myth is that it is an identity marker of the group of tribes who possess this story, indicating some affinity of these tribes with each other. The hardships they had to overcome before they reached their present homeland are comparable to what the Israelites went through in the desert before they reached their promised land.[29] Emergence from a cave (*khul/khur*) as a theory of origin is shared in common among a number of tribes like the Kuki-Chin-Mizos.[30]

---

29. William Shaw, *Notes on the Thadou Kukis* (Kohima: Published on behalf of the Government of Assam, 1929), 24–26; see also T. S. Gangte. *The Kukis of Manipur: A Historical Analysis* (New Delhi: Gyan, 1993): 14–17; Peter Haokip, "Kuki Culture and the Christian Message," unpublished MTh thesis, Jnana Deepa Vidyapeeeth Institute of Philosophy and Religion, Pune, 1979, 3–7.

30. See Khasim Ruivah, "The Tangkhul Nagas," in *Manipur Past and Present: Ordeals and Heritage of a Civilization*, vol. 1, ed. Naorem Sanajaoba (New Delhi: Mittal, 1995): 334–56; Mangthoi Thaimei, "The Rongmeis," in *Manipur: Past and Present*, 378–408; Gangumei Kabui,

Though some myths are not fully documented, the title or the name of the mythical figure can help us find the meaning of the myth. For example in the myth of Galgam, the significance of the name itself provides a clue to the myth's meaning: *Gal* means "war," and *ngam* stands for daring or bravery. The character therefore embodies bravery, chivalry, and strength that can overcome any and every obstacle in life. In short, Galngam is a Kuki "Superman." Similarly in the myths of Moltinchan, Ahsijolneng, and Lenchonghoi, which are stories concerning beauty, the clue to the meaning of the myths lies in the significance of the names of the heroines. The one who coined the name Moltinchan (brightening/lighting up all the hills around) must have been a genius. If we imagine a village in which this girl was living as surrounded by hills and mountains, her beauty made even the surrounding mountains radiant and dazzling. We can say beauty is contagious. This story is in short a myth of beauty which suggests that beautiful people make those around them, people and nature, also beautiful.

Ahsijolneng means friend of *ahsi* (star) which means she is as beautiful and bright as a star. When you convert someone as beautiful as a star into a name for a girl, it becomes Ahshijolneng. There is ingenuity in the creation of such names. The myth of Lenchonghoi is also a myth of beauty because of the love between a sister and her brothers in addition to the motif of brave chivalry. A common feature of these myths is that they are not "happy ever after" stories; they are often punctured with tragedies. Do these tragedies present a negative attitude to life? I would rather say they represent a more realistic picture of life.

I shall now show the possibilities of interpreting a complete myth. In 2013, Jnanadeepa Vidyapeeth of the Pontifical Institute of Philosophy and Religion, Pune, conducted a seminar to commemorate the fiftieth anniversary of the Second Vatican Council of the Catholic Church. The theme was "Faith, Reason, and Wisdom" (*Śraddhā*, *Tarka*, and *Prajñā*). The organizers of the seminar felt that in an age of specialization not only in the field of empirical sciences but also in philosophy and theology, there is a need for an integrating vision, a kind an interdisciplinary endeavour attentive to the diverse voices that cry out to be heard from the various corners of the fragmented world.[31] From the general Indian tradition, the integral approach can be seen from the point of view of faith, reason, and wisdom. I was asked if such an integral approach is

Anal: A Transborder Tribe of Manipur (New Delhi: Mittal, 1985); and Gina Shangkham, "A Brief Account of the Moyons," in *Manipur: Past and Present*, 440–56.

31. See George Kuruvelil, "Editorial," *Jnanadeepa Pune Journal of Religious Studies* 17, no. 1 (January 2014): 3–4.

seen in tribal traditions,[32] and I tried to show that such an integral approach can be seen in the myth of the *dao* sharpener.

The Myth of the *Dao* Sharpener (*Chemtatpa Thusim*)

> One day a man was sharpening his *dao*/knife on a stone by a stream. A shrimp crawled up to him and bit his testicles. Howling in pain, the man sliced off the bamboo nearby. A sliced off bamboo piece flew and hit the cheek of a wild fowl. The wild fowl out of pain scratched the ground and opened up an ant hill full of red ants. The red ants ran helter-skelter and bit the testicles of a sleeping wild boar nearby. The wild boar in pain swung its head wildly cutting off a wild banana plant on which a bat was having a nap. The bat got so startled, it flew off and went right into the ear of an elephant. The elephant got so disturbed that it ran and knocked down the hut of the widow in a nearby hamlet. The widow got so angry she ran off and took shelter by the water source of the village.
>
> When the whole village came to know of what the widow had done, they called a village council meeting and questioned the widow: "Why are you camping at our water source and dirtying it?" they asked.
>
> The widow said, "Because the elephant destroyed my house."
>
> The villagers then summoned the elephant and asked him, "Why did you destroy the widow's hut?"
>
> "Because," the elephant said, "the bat flew into my ear, and I was so disturbed I ran wildly."
>
> Then the bat was summoned and questioned: "Why did you fly into the ear of the elephant?"
>
> The bat said, "Because the wild boar cut down the wild plantain plant on which I was resting, and I had to fly away suddenly."
>
> When the wild boar was questioned, he said, "I was resting peacefully, and suddenly the red ants were all over me, and I had to swing wildly to get rid of them."

32. See Peter Haokip, "Nature, Dynamics and Praxis of the Tiptych: A Tribal Perspective," *Jnanadeepa Pune Journal of Religious Studies* 17, no. 1 (January 2014): 27–41.

The red ants while questioned said, "We too were peacefully inside our home and were disturbed by the wild fowl."

The wild fowl too was questioned by the villagers. In reply it said, "The man with the *dao* sliced off a bamboo which hit my cheek, and I was in terrible pain." And when the man with the *dao* was questioned, he blamed the little shrimp for biting him, causing him to react in pain by slicing off the bamboo.

Finally the shrimp was summoned and questioned. The little shrimp admitted he was the culprit behind the chain of events. He himself suggested the punishment to be meted out to him. He said, "You can either put me back into the stream, in which case I will remain darkish in colour, or boil me alive in water, in which case my appearance will become red and colourful." The villagers decided to put the shrimp in a pot of water to boil him alive. While the shrimp was half-dead on the dry land, it was fully alive in the pot of water and happily jumped out of the pot back into the stream. Shrimps always appear darkish in the water but become red and colourful when boiled to this day.[33]

An Interpretation of the Myth

First of all, this little myth has a truly realistic rural setting, and coming from a rural background, I can really visualize it. Men always carry a *dao*, or knife, when they go to the forest, and a man sharpening his *dao* on a stone by a stream is quite realistic. Beside such streams are found sand stones which are good for sharpening, and men usually select some stones to sharpen their *daos*. If they find a good stone, they carry it home. A stream surrounded by a forest of bamboos, trees, and wild banana plants as the habitat of wild fowls, wild boars, bats, and elephants is also plausible and realistic. A hamlet in the vicinity of such an environment where the hut of a widow at the outskirts of the village is poorly constructed with bamboos and thatch, so becoming an easy target of such mishaps, is also true to reality. At the same time there is an air of artificiality in the myth. Everyone who reads or hears the story will

33. This folktale is a common heritage of many tribes of the Northeast with minor variants. It belongs to the Mizo-Kuki-Chin tribes, and the Nagas and the Karbis, too. See Desmond Kharmawphlang (ed), *Narratives of Northeast India II* (Shillong: PROFRA Publications, 2002), 41. See also B. K. Borgohain and P. C. Chaudhury (eds), *Folk Tales of Nagaland, Manipur, Tripura and Mizoram* (New Delhi: Sterling Publishing, 1991), 19–21; and K. Ghosh and Shukla Ghosh, *Fables and Folk-Tales of Manipur* (Calcutta: Firma KLM, 1998).

know that it is a story created by a wise storyteller to teach some important lessons concerning life. As children we knew this story mostly as a fun story which can be heard at various levels. Nobody knows who the author is, and perhaps nobody bothers about it either. As a Spanish poem says:

> Until the people sing them
> Verses are not really verses;
> And when people sing them
> No one remembers their authors.[34]

Second, the myth demonstrates the dynamic, mutual interaction of reason, faith, and wisdom. The solution to a problem that has occurred in the hamlet is seen in the holistic aspect in which wisdom seems to be the guiding force. Wisdom stands in the middle as it were to draw from both faith and reason a resolution to the crisis in the community. Wisdom calls on the community to see the rationality of the events and invites them to have faith in the reasonableness of the accounts given by the characters and accept it. Wisdom is the foundation on which traditional societies live and conduct their daily lives. Though not always obvious, it is embedded in the authentic traditional institutions, practices, and myths. It has a particular concern for the widow who suffered most in the story, as she often does in real life as well. The resolution of the crisis is set in motion because the widow is deprived of the bare minimum she had.

The chain of events that took place as narrated by the characters in terms of spontaneous reactions to the pain and discomfort they experienced seems reasonable (reason). The sincerity of their account is accepted and believed by the village council (faith). The result emerges through the wisdom of the deliberations of the village council. It is clear that the characters starting from the *dao* sharpener did not act intentionally. The one guilty of initiating the chain of events was the shrimp, but it is not clear whether he acted intentionally. Even if he had, it is clear that he could never have foreseen the whole chain of events. He could not really be accused of being guilty, yet he admitted he was the culprit and suggested a punishment for himself which cunningly contained an escape.

We can assume that the village council took place by the site of the village water source which was occupied by the worst affected victim, the widow.

34. Manuel y Antonio Machado, *Obras Completas*, quoted in Louis Alonso Schökel, *The Inspired Word: Scripture in the Light of Language and Literature* (New York: Herder and Herder, 1965), 229–30.

Probably it was the same stream by which the man was sharpening his *dao*. The little shrimp is a water creature and must have been half-dead out of the water for the duration of the meeting. Hence, as soon as he was put into the pot to be boiled according to his own instructions, he must have got back his strength and was gladly able to jump back into the water of the stream. This is what happens when a community in crisis comes together with reasonableness, faith, and wisdom. Any problem is solvable.

There may be other ways of interpreting this story. Although as children we were told this story as an amusing tale, it can be also understood in terms of the human tendency to play the blame game as it often is today. We tend to blame someone else for our actions instead of owning up ourselves. Hemkholun Haokip, in his BD thesis "Myths as Sources for Doing Tribal Theology," interpreted the same story in terms of the "interrelatedness and interdependence with one another of humans, animals, birds, and nature. They share equality and mutual respect for each other."[35] In fact, tribal culture in general has been broadly described as including "extraordinary values of solidarity with nature, egalitarianism, a non-competitive collaboration with one another, and a filial (not mercantile) relationship with the land."[36] This is true of Kuki culture; traditional Kukis lived in the midst of forests, and their life was a constant interaction with the forces of nature, and hence a harmonious co-existence with nature was of prime importance. The interconnectedness of the Kuki life with the environment is nowhere seen more clearly than in their practice of shifting cultivation.[37]

Other myths known as etiological myths describe the origin of things. For example, a myth about why the crow is black relates that the crow was in charge of decorating all the other birds. It generously decorated all its fellow birds with beautiful colours, but at the end no colour remained, so the crow is black. When people do all things for others and there is nothing left for themselves, they are compared to a crow.

Another small myth tells why today the python is without poison. In the beginning the python was the most poisonous snake in the world. One day it bit a man and he died instantly. But the python did not know it and sent an

35. Hemkholun Haokip, "Myth as Sources for Doing Tribal Theology, with Special Reference to the Kuki Tribes of Manipur," unpublished BD thesis, John Roberts Theological Seminary, Shillong, 2005, 32.

36. George M. Soares-Prabhu, "Tribal Values in India," *Jeevadhara* 24, no. 140 (March 1994): 84.

37. Peter Haokip, "Eco-Theology and Spirituality: A Perspective of Kuki Tribe," *Oriens Journal for Contextual Theology* 3 (2012): 78.

emissary, the tiny red ant, to the man's village to ascertain whether the man had died or not. The tiny, cunning red ant had his own plans. He obediently went to the village and saw the man dead alright, laid beside the main pillar of the house (*sutpi*) in ceremonial dress and surrounded by the whole village in mourning, according to traditional Kuki custom. But when the red ant came back to the python and was asked to report, he told the python, "My dear python, the man you bit is not dead at all. On the contrary, he is dressed up in ceremonial dress and the whole village is having a grand celebration." The python was so furious and frustrated with himself that he spilled all his deadly poison on the ground, and the tiny red ants swarmed in the spilled poison. That is why today the python has no poison, but if the little red ant bites you, it is very painful.

Conclusion

Mythical narratives may not always convey meanings that are positive and contribute to social well-being. For example, some storytellers have attempted to use Kuki myths to suggest that the Kuki-Chin-Mizo peoples are descendants of the ten lost tribes of Israel, perhaps a form of modern myth making we could do without? However, this chapter has shown both the importance of myth to the identity and values of tribal peoples and the messages they contain for the wider human family today. It is to be hoped that work will continue to ensure the collection and preservation of this precious cultural heritage before it becomes too late. We have to do whatever we can to make our rich cultural heritage occupy its rightful place in our lives and in our hearts. The poetic language of traditional myth and song is in real danger of disappearing, and the loss of a language involves the removal of a culture and a unique source of knowledge of the world and the human condition. Our responsibility is enormous. So let me end with the immortal words of Robert Frost:

> The woods are lovely, dark and deep
> But I have promises to keep,
> And miles to go before I sleep,
> And miles to go before I sleep.[38]

The woods of the Kuki cultural heritage are really lovely, dark, and deep, but we have promises to keep before we sleep.

38. Robert Frost, *The Concise Oxford Dictionary of Quotations* (Oxford: Oxford University Press, 1981), 103.

10

The Relevance of Spirit Consciousness for Tribal Christians in Northeast India

Elungkiebe Zeliang

The belief that God created humans as both physical and spiritual beings has meant that Christians have historically been concerned for both peoples' physical welfare and their spiritual well-being. This concern has led people to relate with the unseen spiritual powers which have been a factor in the rise of many religious traditions in the world. Indigenous peoples, identified as "tribals" in the Indian context, number between and 380 and-500 million people globally.[1] They share similar religious traditions which, while locally specific and distinctive, recognise spirit consciousness as a common hallmark. The tribal peoples of Northeast India possess their own local traditions in which this "primal" belief in the reality of the spirit world plays a central role. As discussed elsewhere in this book, both Hinduism and Christianity have been introduced into this area, with many people living on the plains becoming Hindu while Christianity won converts among the tribes in the hill regions. In both cases, the missionaries have needed to interact with traditional beliefs which, as other contributors have shown, remain present both among converts

1. Indigenous peoples/tribals are found in over ninety countries around the world. Of the global population, they are only about 5 percent, but about 15 percent of the poorest. "Indigenous Peoples," World Bank, (19 March 2021), https://www.worldbank.org/en/topic/indigenous peoples. Retrieved 16/02/2022

and those tribal people who continue to practice indigenous religion, often in movements embracing reform of various kinds.

The study of tribal religious traditions suggests that they have many similarities with Christian beliefs, and converts have discovered significant points of contact between the worldviews which underlie the Bible and their own concerns with the realm of the spirit. Conversion did not eliminate their sense of the reality of that realm. In fact in becoming Christian and gaining access to the Gospels, converts frequently recognize in Christ answers to questions emerging from within their traditional worldview. The fact that the Bible presents Jesus as the victor over all other spiritual powers has caused Christianity to be recognized as responding to urgent contextual issues and has drastically reduced the fear of evil spirits among the tribal Christians. In this chapter and as a tribal Christian myself, I argue that the tradition of tribal spirit consciousness is compatible with the teaching of the Bible and is relevant for tribal Christians. The study is an exploratory discussion from a tribal-historical perspective based on available literature, personal experiences and observations, and a small empirical survey.

The Context of Northeast India

The social and political context of this region has been surveyed in detail elsewhere in this book, so here I offer only additional facts relevant to this study. The term "tribe" has been critiqued as being pejorative and inaccurate. Despite this the fact remains that without defining it, the government of India identifies indigenous, ethnic groups throughout the country as "Scheduled Tribes" in Article 342 of the Indian Constitution. In a consultation held in Shillong in 1962, tribal leaders from across India agreed on a definition of "tribe" as "an indigenous, homogenous unit, speaking a common language, claiming a common ancestry, living in a particular geographical area, backward in technology, preliterate, loyally observing social and political customs based on kinship."[2] According to the 2011 census, the population of the Scheduled Tribes in India as a whole is 104 million, which amounts to 8.6 percent of the country's total population. These groups are scattered across thirty states and

2. Quoted in Jonathan Thumra, "The Primal Religious Tradition," in *Religious Traditions of India*, eds. Daniel, Scott and Singh (Delhi: ISPCK, 2001), 46. It is surprising that the technologies of tribal societies are described as "backward" rather than, say, "simple." The same applies regarding the term "preliterate" which suggests the inevitability of the shift to a literate culture and thus devalues orality. [Editorial comment].

are found especially in forest and hill areas. A total of 705 ethnic groups have been recognized as Scheduled Tribes throughout the country.[3]

In the Northeast, tribes can be distinguished in various ways. *Geographically* they are either plains or hill tribes. This distinction is not absolute, especially today when migration patterns erode such neat distinctions, but for example the Bodos, Karbis, Mising, Rabha, and others live on the plains of Assam, while the Nagas are found in the hills of Aranachul, Assam, Manipur, and Nagaland. A further distinction is *social structures* since some tribes are matrilineal while others are patrilineal, or patriarchal. In the former, the lineage passes through the female line, and the youngest daughter inherits the major share of the ancestral property. In the latter, male members have rights of inheritance, and generally the eldest son is the main beneficiary while the youngest gets the parental home. A third distinction is the *political systems*. Some groups practice monarchical patterns of government in which hereditary chieftains are vested with decisive powers, while others follow a system of gerontocracy in which village councils composed of nominated elders are responsible for local administration. A further distinction, of course, is *languages*, for large numbers of linguistic traditions exist throughout the region.

What we have described here are the *traditional* patterns and structures of the peoples of the Northeast. But in the contemporary situation, modern development, urbanization, and patterns of migration are changing the once stable tribal societies as significant numbers of people from elsewhere in India have moved into the Northeast, while many local people, especially those who are young and educated, move in the opposite direction. It is the purpose of this chapter to reflect on precisely the extent to which the changes resulting from such population movements may be impacting traditional cultures, and especially the perception of spiritual powers and the spiritual world.

God and the Spirits in Tribal Religions and Societies

Scholars have given the religious traditions of the tribal peoples different names at different times. In the nineteenth century, the term "animism" was widely used[4] and together with the phrase "primitive religion" reflected the influence of evolutionary understandings of the history of religion. More recently

3. C. Chandramouli, "Scheduled tribes in India as revealed in census 2011," Census of India 2011 (3 May 2013) https//:trbal.nic.in/ST/3-STinindiaascensus2011_compressed.pdf.

4. Sir Edward B. Tylor first propounded the theory of animism. G. van der Leeuw, *Religion in Essence and Manifestation* (London: Allen and Unwin, 1963).

these traditions have been called preliterate, primal, or tribal religions.[5] The tribal people of Northeast India practice indigenous religions passed down orally from one generation to the next. According to Jonathan H. Thumra, a renowned tribal religious scholar, the main features of these tribal religions are belief in the Supreme Being, spirits, *mana*, fetishism, taboo, totemism, omens and divination, magic, the evil eye, life after death, and the role of religious functionaries.[6] This chapter is limited to traditional beliefs concerning the Supreme Being and the spirits.

All tribal people in the region believe in the existence of the Supreme Being who is the ultimate authority. Traditional names for God sometimes suggest a feminine deity while others point toward maleness. It is possible to list local names for God with feminine endings and then to find other languages in which the opposite is the case. However, as Jangkholam Haokip points out elsewhere in this book, these names may suggest that God transcends the distinction between the sexes, being far beyond the human condition. There is no doubt that the tribal people believe God to be the creator and sustainer of all things. At the same time, the deity does not interfere in the daily affairs of the people, and worship and thanksgiving to God is limited to crucial transitions and experiences in life including childbirth, marriage, death, or a bumper harvest, etc.[7]

However, God is believed to be all powerful, ever present, and the final judge of all people. Writing about the Konyak's belief in God as the one who sees and judges people, the German anthropologist Christoph von Furer-Haimendorf writes, "If a man told a blatant lie, one of the bystanders might call out, 'You are lying. *Gawang* [God] sees it and will tear your mouth.'"[8] Likewise, traditional people resign themselves to God in perplexing situations and appeal for divine judgment in contexts of injustice. For instance the Aos say, "*Tsüngremi dang metet!*" (God only knows!), and almost identical phrases are found in many other local languages.

5. Thumra, "Primal Religious Tradition," 45–46; A. Wati Longchar, *The Tribal Religious Traditions in North East India: An Introduction* (Jorhat: self-published, 2000), 5–8.

6. Thumra, "Primal Religious Tradition," 47–73.

7. Thumra, "Primal Religious Tradition," 48–49; A. Peihwang Wangsa, "The Traditional Concept of Supreme Being, (Youngwan Kahwang)" in Garnering Tribal Resources for Doing Tribal Christian Theology, Razouselie Lasetso [ed] (Jorhat: Eastern Theological College, 2008), 230–231, 230–31.

8. Christoph von Furer-Haimendorf, *The Konyak Nagas: An Indian Frontier Tribe* (New York: Hoff Ringchart and Winston, 1968), 101.

How then is this belief in the Creator God related to the role of the many spirits who continually impact daily life, as suggested earlier? In the nineteenth century, British colonial observers were struck by the traditional perception of the spirit world, as can be seen in the verdict of the Political Agent of Manipur, W. McCulloch, who said that local people believed "in the existence of many other deities" who were assigned "to the highest peaks or great crags impracticable to the climber."[9] McCulloch failed to differentiate between the benevolent and malevolent spirits and assumed all of them to be evil and in need of being propitiated. However, the distinction between benevolent and malevolent spirits is very important in traditional religion. There are tutelary spirits of the village, clan, and family; spirits that provide and protect crops; and ancestral spirits, all of whom are benevolent. On the other hand are spirits that exist in the cliffs, rivers, forests, and lakes which are believed to harm people, to cause sickness or death, and to bring about calamities.

While the Supreme Being does not interfere in the daily life of the people, the spirits, both benevolent and malevolent, are believed to be continually active and so demand attention. The protection and favour of benevolent spirits is sought through incantations and rituals, and they are thanked for good health, bumper harvests, and success in hunting or warfare.[10] By contrast, the malevolent spirits require appeasement through sacrifices (*ratak* in Zeme; *inthawina* in Mizo[11]), and since sickness is believed to be caused by offending such spirits, appeasing sacrifices to the malevolent spirits are performed when the situation demands.

The primal sense of the reality of the spirit world is related to the traditional understanding of what has come to be called the "natural world." That is to say in contrast to the modern view of the non-human creation, which assumes the world to be *disenchanted,* devoid of "spirit," and so vulnerable to human desires and greed, in the tribal worldview there is no strict dichotomy between the secular and the sacred. It is believed that spirits indwell the natural world so that animals and plants demand respect. As Lal Ngurauva observes, "all trees of the size of a full-grown Mizo dog (which is small in size) except one kind of tree called *Thing Thiang*, were believed to have their spirits."[12] Before cutting down a large tree, a tribal person will show his respect by saying, "You

9. W. McCulloch, *Valley of Manipur* (Delhi: Gian Publications 1980 [1859]), 54.

10. See Thumra, "Primal Religious Tradition," 49.

11. Mangkhosat Kipgen, *Christianity and Mizo Culture* (Aizawl: Mizo Theological Conference, 1996), 111.

12. Lal Ngurauva quoted in Kipgen, *Christianity and Mizo Culture*, 107.

may be older than me, but I am going to cut you down today for my use."[13] Large animals like tigers or reptiles like the python are believed to have spirits which need to be handled with care. So if a tiger is killed, the men of the village will return in full armour with howls and cries to bring the hunted animal into the village so that the spirit of the tiger might not harm the villagers.[14] Consequently, it becomes clear that the spirit consciousness of the tribal people shapes and impacts their lives in a multitude of ways.

A further example is ethical. Honesty and the avoidance of blatant lies, or of the theft of property, is underpinned by the knowledge of the spirit world and the belief that retribution for misbehaviour will come from that world. This same sense of the sacredness of the rest of the created world results in a closeness to nature and the avoidance of intentional damage or exploitation of animals, plants, or the earth itself. People live by hunting, fishing, and cultivation, but these activities are accompanied by due respect to all living creatures and the avoidance of the rampant killing of animals when they pose no harm to the community and no threat to crops. Spirit consciousness also impacts human relationships. For example, deformed or disabled people are not mocked or marginalized for fear of offending God who is their creator. More generally, tribal communities practice compassion by extending physical, material, and moral support to each other in times of need. The Zeme expression *mina dui nrau mede hera dui nrau* (even if one does not respect humans out of respect for God/spirit) demonstrates the compassionate solidarity which flows from a worldview in which both God and the spirits hear and see everything and are revered.

Spirit Consciousness in a Changing World

In the modern history of India and the Northeast, two developments have massively impacted the tribal peoples and have brought new challenges to their traditional way of life and its underlying, foundational beliefs, including the spirit consciousness with which this chapter is concerned. Since the nineteenth century, the primary agents of change in the region have been the Western political and economic systems introduced by the British accompanied by the introduction of modern forms of education and scientific medicine. Following the Treaty of Yandabo, signed by the British imperial power and

13. Personal interview with Loli Kape, Shillong, 23 May 2019.

14. In the 1980s, I experienced how the village men with gun shots and howls brought a hunted tiger into the village.

the Myanmar king in 1826, the Northeast formally came under colonial rule. Beginning from Assam, the British gradually extended their rule to all areas of the region by the end of the century. They introduced a new political system, enforced by a standing armed force and police service, together with new legal powers, a prison system, and an administrative hierarchy. The imported politics undermined the traditional authority of chieftainship and the village heads in tribal societies, while the introduction of a money economy and the concept of wage earning employment brought tremendous changes to erstwhile tribal societies.

The introduction of Western education and modern medicine had a major role in the decline of spirit consciousness among the tribal peoples. The colonial power collaborated with Christian missions in the field of education by providing grant-in-aid to the mission schools. Education was entrusted to the Welsh Presbyterians among the Khasis and Jaintias from the 1850s and to American Baptists among the Garos a decade later. Missions appeared subsequently across the region, and Roman Catholics established many schools and colleges in the Northeast. Hospitals and dispensaries were established at the same time, bringing Western scientific medicine to a people who had traditionally regarded illness as having both social and spiritual dimensions. Inevitably the clash of worldviews triggered by the expansion of Western education and modern medicine engendered modifications in the tribal spirit consciousness.

The second major agent of change across the Northeast was the spread of Christianity. Portuguese Roman Catholics made contact with people in Assam as early as the seventeenth century, but it was British colonial rule which opened the way for Protestant missions to enter the region during the nineteenth century. British and American Baptists and Welsh Presbyterians were followed by German Salvatorians led by Fr. Otto Hopfenmueller in Shillong in 1890. These Western missionaries introduced the tribal peoples to the gospel and saw an extraordinary response which resulted in significant movements of conversion. The question to be asked is whether given their association with Western education and medicine, and the link between missions and colonial power, the Christianization of large numbers of the tribal peoples was also a secularizing factor which diminished spirit consciousness and eroded traditional values? Or did Christianity enable converts to make the transition into the modern world while *retaining* a central belief in the sacred because the new faith has many points of contact with the old traditions, even though these went frequently unnoticed by Western missionaries?

We cannot answer these critical questions here. However, in order to assess the current situation with respect to spirit consciousness among young people in the region, I conducted a survey of one hundred students at Martin Luther Christian University in Shillong, all of them between the ages of nineteen and twenty-seven years old. The nature of this group is significant because this generation is exposed both to education at university level and to urban culture beyond the confines of traditional life in village settings. Participants were asked to respond to nine questions related to their beliefs concerning the existence and influence of the world of spirits. The results included the following findings:

- 86 percent believed in the existence of good and bad spirits;
- 70 percent believed that the spirits monitor both words and deeds;
- 51 percent believed that the spirits cause sickness;
- 49 percent believed in demon possession – but 51 percent rejected this belief or were unsure;
- 26 percent believed malign spirits should be appeased – 73 percent said they should not;
- 96 percent affirmed that Jesus Christ has superiority over all spirit powers.

The findings of this survey suggest some significant shifts in the perception of young people in relation to traditional spirit consciousness. While the reality of the spirit world was strongly affirmed, the expansion of education, advancement in medical science, and Christianization have led to questioning belief in the power of spirits, while the faith that Jesus has authority over all spirits explains the diminishing fear of malign forces of evil.

Challenges and Opportunities for Tribal Christian Theology

The changes we have described as commencing in the nineteenth century have continued and indeed accelerated in the intervening years. On the one hand, the era of Christian missions based in Europe and North America is over, and Christianity appears to be in deepening crisis in the Western world. On the other hand, the forces of secularization and the growth of a global economy of free market capitalism have increased until they have become an ideology which impacts peoples everywhere on earth, including the tribal population of India. In this context, how might tribal Christians respond in ways which reconnect them to neglected elements of traditional culture, not simply to preserve ancient traditions, but because when brought to the feet of the crucified Christ and offered to him as the Lord of all worlds, they have something positive and vital to offer toward the healing of the brokenness of the world in the twenty-first century?

Perhaps the unique feature of the revelation of God in the Bible concerns the mystery of the Trinity: one God in three persons. God the Father appears and speaks to people in different situations, revealing himself as Creator and as the Liberator who sets slaves free and enters into a covenant of grace which demands of his worshippers justice and justice alone. Although he chose one people to serve and love him, it is clear that from the very beginning, his ultimate purpose was to extend grace to every nation and tribe on earth, and that his divine intention is to bring *shalom* to the whole created world. When the Bible was translated into local languages, the name used for God was invariably the one found in traditional myths concerning creation, so that the new revelation of God the Father had a direct link with the Supreme Being of tribal traditions through the centuries past. God whom tribal people do not believe interferes in the daily affairs of people moved into the very centre of life with the promise that as our heavenly Father, he knows our needs and cares intimately for us. The tribal Christian leader Rabi Pame asserts that the traditional concept of the Supreme Being prepared the minds of the Zeme people to accept without struggle "the Christian monotheistic God."[15] This preparation can be further illustrated by the way people respond to God in situations of distress, perplexity, or grief in the context of mourning. The Zeme, Mizo, and Kuki people all have phrases which express submission to the will of God, while by contrast and for example, they attribute a happy married life to the Supreme Being whom they acknowledge as the one who "knotted the couple's hair." In the case of an unsuccessful marriage, the Zeme say, "*Hera tamtok kega*" (lack of knotting the couple's hair by God) and accept the subsequent divorce.

At the heart of the Christian story is the message of the incarnation and the revelation of the very being of God in the person of Jesus Christ. As we see in the results of the survey of students above, whatever differences they had in attitudes toward the spirit world, there was almost unanimity in their belief that Jesus has power over all other spirits of the world. This belief seems to reflect a contextualized Christology, since a central focus on the supremacy of the crucified and risen Jesus over the unseen realm of spiritual powers was not a feature of Western missionary preaching. Once the Bible became available

15. Rabi Pame, *Culture and the Church: History of Zeme Naga Church N. C. Hills, Assam* (Nzauna: Nzauna Baptist Church, 1995), 78.

in their own tongues, tribal converts to Christianity could discover aspects of the gospel story which missionaries had overlooked, but which were vital elements of the "good news" in their traditional context. At the same time a critical issue relating to conversion has to be considered. How has it come about that while tribal peoples possess what might be called "the fear of God," which makes them very careful in both words and deeds, contemporary society in which punishment from God or the spirits is no longer feared is marred by growing social problems including corruption, injustice, and sexual crimes, among other antisocial actions? Is the tribal belief in God as all-knowing and the final judge not compatible with the sovereignty of the Lord according to Psalm 139:2–12? And does not Paul's teaching that our bodies are the temple of the Holy Spirit (1 Cor 6:19–20) require that Christians live self-disciplined and honest lives in solidarity and love for one another?

Finally, the gospel message includes the revelation of the Holy Spirit who came like a mighty wind and filled the believers on the day of Pentecost (Acts 2:1–4). The first Christian communities experienced a new spiritual reality and received spiritual gifts which enabled them to confront the malignant spiritual powers which were part of their world, and to live together in communities which reflected the example of the life of Jesus. Tribal Christians have realized that the biblical accounts testify that there are real spiritual beings who work against God and bring suffering to the world. Nevertheless, the Bible affirms God's ultimate control, and the Gospels present Jesus as confronting and overcoming all evil powers. Christ gave his disciples "authority to drive out impure spirits and to heal every disease and sickness" (Matt. 10:1), while the apostle Paul recognized the spiritual dimensions of our struggle "against the rulers, against the authorities, against the powers of this dark world and against the spiritual forces of evil in the heavenly realms" (Eph. 6:12).

Conclusion

We have seen how the tribal societies of Northeast India have been undergoing tremendous change since the coming of the British colonial power and of Western Christian missions in the nineteenth century. This transformation has affected traditional political and socioeconomic life. But the work of missionaries has also resulted in religious change as Christianity made rapid progress, especially among the hill tribes, so that today many tribes in the region are fully Christianized. However, my study revealed that most tribal Christians retain a high spirit consciousness, and although most reject the traditional practice of appeasing evil spirits, they continue to believe that these invisible powers cause sickness and may possess people. The belief that Jesus is the Victor over all spiritual powers is of crucial importance in relation to the context we have described, since this belief relates closely to the realities of the traditional worldview while also providing a foundation on which a contextual theology can recognize the compatibility of the gospel with many aspects of indigenous knowledge. At the same time, such a theology will enable tribal Christians to share their wisdom with the wider world.

For further information on this topic, see the following:

Elungkiebe Zeliang, *Pioneer Missionaries of North East India* (Jorhat: Eastern Theological College, 2003).

———, *A History of the Manipur Baptist Convention* (Imphal: Manipur Baptist Convention, 2005).

———, *Charismatic Movements in the Baptist Churches of North East India* (Delhi: ISPCK, 2014).

11

The Emergence of World Christianity and Its Implications for Indigenous Peoples

David W. Smith

My task in this chapter is to reflect on the significance of the emergence of "world Christianity" for peoples belonging to, or deeply influenced by, traditional cultures and religions. While our immediate concern is with the "tribal" areas of Northeast India, the type of religion which shaped this region prior to the impact of Christianity and modernity is found on every continent and has played a highly significant role in the growth and eventual transformation of the Christian faith across the past two centuries.

Following Andrew Walls, I am going to refer to these traditions as "primal," both because this term avoids the negative implications of language used in the past by Western scholars and missionaries and because as Walls says, the traditional beliefs and practices of small-scale societies throughout the world "underlie all other faiths, and often exist in symbiosis with them, continuing . . . to have an active life within and around cultures and communities influenced by those faiths."[1] Walls goes on to say that what are often described as the major world religions – Hinduism, Buddhism, Christianity, and Islam – are

1. Andrew Walls, "Primal Religious Traditions in Today's World," in *Religion in Today's World*, ed. Frank Whaling (Edinburgh: T&T Clark, 1987), 250. This chapter is reprinted in Andrew F. Walls, *The Missionary Movement in Christian History: Studies in the Transmission of Faith* (New York: Orbis, 1996), 119–39.

subsequent to the primal traditions, and therefore believers within those religions, "and for that matter non-believers, are primalists underneath."[2]

The Modern Missionary Movement and Indigenous Peoples

Historians have identified a series of stages, or paradigms, in the two-thousand-year story of Christianity in which the movement has been shaped by the particular cultural contexts within which it has successively taken root. The period which witnessed the emergence of Christian missions, both Catholic and Protestant, has been described as the age of *expanding Europe*. This expansion involved the spread of the economic and political power of European nations across the globe, and the movement of huge numbers of European people to the southern hemisphere, so that by the twentieth century, "people of European origin occupied, possessed, or dominated the greater part of the globe."[3]

The concurrence of expanding Western political and economic power with the missionary movement is reflected in William Carey's famous *Enquiry into the Obligations of Christians to Use Means for the Conversion of the Heathens* of 1792. He comments on the way representatives of British commercial interests "cross the widest and most tempestuous seas, and encounter the most unfavourable climates" in their quest for profit and financial gain, and then calls upon Christians to show an even greater zeal to extend the kingdom of God throughout the world.[4] Carey and his colleagues displayed genuine sensitivity with regard to the cultures and religions of Asia. This sensitivity is reflected in the fact that their printing press at Serampore was used not only to produce Christian literature, but also to publish the great Hindu epics and translations of the works of Confucius. The Serampore missionaries stated that their objectives were "not the changing of names, the dress, the food, and the innocent usages of mankind," but rather "a moral and divine change in the hearts and conduct of men."[5] Nonetheless, both Catholic and Protestant missionaries were shaped by the long history of Christendom, so their expression of the gospel inevitably

2. Walls, "Primal Religious Traditions," 252.

3. Walls, *Missionary Movement*, 21.

4. William Carey, *An Enquiry into the Obligations of Christians to Use Means for the Conversion of the Heathens* (Didcot: Baptist Missionary Society, 1991 [1792]), 109.

5. This quotation is from the famous "Form of Agreement" contained in the Baptist Missionary Society *Periodical Accounts*, vol. 3 (1806), 208.

took a Western form and frequently "seemed inseparable from the categories of European life and thought."[6]

This shaping was especially the case with regard to European attitudes toward traditional, primal religions. Edmund Leach describes how, from about 1840, the new academic discipline of anthropology emerged in Britain, led by scholars who "rejected the unity of mankind postulated in the Bible in favour of a theory that there are a variety of man-like species *of which only the white-skinned European is a fully rational human being.*"[7]Later in the nineteenth century with the development of social Darwinism, negative attitudes toward primal peoples and their beliefs hardened to such an extent that they came to be described as "living fossils"; survivals from an earlier stage of evolution who, to quote Leach, reveal "the stupidity and depravity of the beast-like behaviour of our primeval ancestors."[8]

Western missionaries of course retained the biblical insistence on the unity of the human race. As a result there are many examples of missionary encounters with non-Western traditions which resulted in the need to reflect on previously unknown theological issues and created an increasingly critical perspective on the missionary's own culture. Not infrequently this reflection led to serious tensions between missionaries and their compatriots in an era of imperial self-confidence and civilizational arrogance.[9] David Livingstone, who became a genuinely iconic figure in Victorian Britain, experienced another kind of tension when, in the heart of Africa, he met and challenged a traditional rainmaker who refuted the suggestion that his practice should give way to Western medicine. Here is an account of the rainmaker's contribution to this conversation:

---

6. Andrew Walls, *The Cross-Cultural Process in Christian History* (Edinburgh: T&T Clark, 2002), 49.

7. Edmund Leach, *Social Anthropology* (Glasgow: Fontana Paperbacks, 1982), 15, emphasis added. Leach goes on to say that this "new arrogant and ethnocentric science . . . fitted perfectly with the ethos of the era of European colonial expansion and the westward movement of the American Frontier, for it rested on the basic premise that all non-Europeans are stupid, childish, barbarous and servile by their very nature," 16.

8. Leach, *Social Anthropology*, 17.

9. For an early example, see the extraordinary account of the French Protestant Jean de Lery whose life-transforming experiences among the Tupinamba Indians in Brazil are movingly described in his *History of a Voyage to the Land of Brazil*, trans. and ed. Janet Whatley (Berkeley: University of California Press, 1990). I have discussed Jean de Lery in "The Forgotten 'Grandfather' of Protestant Mission: Perspectives on Globalization from Jean de Lery," *Missiology* 34, no. 3 (July 2006): 349–59.

> I use my medicines and you employ yours; we are both doctors, and doctors are not deceivers. You give a patient medicine. Sometimes God is pleased to heal him by means of your medicine: sometimes not – he dies. When he is cured, you take credit of what God does. I do the same. Sometimes God grants us rain, sometimes not. When he does, we take the credit of the charm. When a patient dies, you don't give up trust in your medicine, neither do I when rain fails. If you wish me to leave off my medicines, why continue your own?[10]

Lamin Sanneh concludes that the Western missionary had been challenged "in the deepest recesses of trust and faith" and was compelled to ask himself why, as a man of faith, he had "come to repose so much trust in modern medicine"?[11]

The answer to that question, of course, is that Livingstone, like all the missionaries at this time, was profoundly influenced by the European Enlightenment, by a belief in the advanced nature of Western civilization, and by a sense of historical destiny to spread this superior culture around the world alongside the gospel of Christ. Jangkholam Haokip's study of the history of Christian evangelisation in Northeast India, and especially among the Kuki, shows how a negative view of primal cultures combined with a theology which stressed individual conversion created a crisis of identity which continues today.

> Conversion, understood within a Western worldview as involving individuals embracing faith without reference to the traditional bonds of kinship and community, resulted in new forms of spirituality and theology which do not take into consideration issues of the people's identity and existence as a group in a multi-ethnic context.[12]

---

10. Lamin Sanneh, *Translating the Message: The Missionary Impact on Culture* (New York: Orbis Books, 1989), 163.

11. Sanneh, 163.

12. Jangkholam Haokip, *Can God Save My Village? A Theological Study of Identity among the Tribal People of North-East India with a Special Reference to the Kukis of Manipur* (Carlisle: Langham Monographs, 2014), 222. The stand out example of a Western missionary learning how to adapt the presentation of the gospel in the context of a primal society is Vincent Donovan's wonderful study of his work among the Masai people of East Africa. He describes in detail what it meant to approach a community as "a homogeneous group of people that considers itself a living, social organism, distinct from other social groups." He writes that, "no individual adult Masai would have agreed to participate in a lengthy, ordered dialogue and discussion between the Masai culture and the Christian message. He agreed to take this step only within the framework of his community, with his community, bringing his relations and relationships with him." Vincent Donovan, *Christianity Rediscovered: An Epistle from the Masai* (London: SCM, 1978), 84.

Mission after Christendom

The era of expanding Europe is now part of history, as is the Western missionary movement which accompanied it. In its place we live in a postcolonial, globalised world in which, to the surprise of many people, Christianity has entered an entirely new phase in its history with the emergence of what has come to be called "world Christianity."[13] In a remarkably perceptive book published as long ago as 1968, the late Kenneth Cragg wrote that Christianity would have "to die to the possessiveness of Western forms in order live authentically within the fullness of human cultures." He continues,

> As the Christ of Galilee and Jerusalem in New Testament times became the Christ of the Mediterranean, of Athens and Rome, so the Christ of the West must be more evidently the Christ of the world. It is the conviction of Christian faith that He is only known anywhere in His fullness, when the whole world, in its cultural diversity, takes possession of Him and in freedom, in thought and in form, tells of Him what it learns and loves.[14]

The shift within the world Christian movement during the past decades involves not only a *geographical* relocation, since the numerical growth of Christianity has occurred across the southern hemisphere, but also a *social* transformation in that the vast majority of professing Christians are now to be found in areas of deprivation and economic hardship, within the margins of a globalised world. This shift is highly significant because it represents a return to the pattern of mission which we discover on the pages of the New Testament, where the gospel was carried from the margins of empire to the centre of imperial power by people who lacked status and honour. As the World Council of Churches' document "Together Towards Life" puts it, "Mission has been understood as a movement taking place from the centre to the periphery, and from the privileged to the marginalized of society. Now people at the

---

13. There has been a veritable explosion of publications dealing with this phenomenon. See for example, Lamin Sanneh and Michael McClymond, eds., *The Wiley Blackwell Companion to World Christianity* (Chichester: John Wiley, 2016); and with regard to theology, William Dyrness and Velli-Matti Karkkainen, eds., *Global Dictionary of Theology* (Downers Grove, IL: IVP Academic, 2008).

14. Kenneth Cragg, *Christianity in World Perspective* (London: Lutterworth, 1968), 193, 195.

margins are claiming their key role as agents of mission and affirming mission as transformation."[15]

This same document goes on to affirm the "testimonies of peoples whose traditions have been scorned and mocked by theologians and scientists," but whose ancient wisdom provides the world with "the vital and sometimes new orientation that can connect us again with the life of the Spirit in creation."[16] In other words, the *primal* traditions, dismissed in the nineteenth century as mere superstition, are being rediscovered both by Christians within such societies and by people in the West who increasingly recognise the catastrophe toward which a rationalist worldview is propelling both the human family and the created world.

Primal Traditions and World Christianity

As the awareness of the gravity of the global ecological crisis increases, critical questions are increasingly heard concerning the ideology of the free market and the belief that the development of nations and peoples requires a commitment to continuous economic growth. The theological critique of such dogmas has been led by liberation theologians in Latin America who developed a critical hermeneutic from below and read the Bible as the record of God's struggle to bring *shalom* to a broken world. However, there is evidence of a remarkable change in this tradition as the ecological systems which make life on this planet possible are seen to be in danger of collapse. Theologians in Latin America have turned toward the ancient wisdom of the tribal peoples in the Amazon rainforests and elsewhere. This turn is reflected in the title of Leonardo Boff's book *Cry of the Earth, Cry of the Poor.* He writes,

> Humankind may find itself facing violence and destruction at levels never seen before on the face of the Earth unless we collectively decide to change the course of civilization and shift its thrust from the logic of means at the service of an exclusionary accumulation toward a logic of ends serving the well-being of

15. World Council of Churches, "Together Towards Life: Mission and Evangelism in Changing Landscapes," in *Ecumenical Visions for the 21st Century: A Reader for Theological Education,* eds. Melisande Lorke and Dietrich Werner (Geneva: World Council of Churches, 2013), 192.

16. "Together Towards Life," 195.

> planet Earth, of human beings, and of all beings in the exercise of freedom and cooperation among all peoples.[17]

Boff discusses what he calls "the permanent message of original peoples" and acknowledges that such groups are to be found everywhere on earth and possess a wisdom capable of showing "how we can be human, indeed profoundly human, without having to pass through the critical rationality of modernity or through the process of dominating the Earth as in the schemes of technology." He concludes that at a point at which our civilization is in grave crisis, "we want to listen to the permanent message of the native people."[18]

Even more remarkable is Pablo Richard's discussion of "indigenous biblical hermeneutics." Having spent six years working with the Kunas Indians in Panama, listening to their traditional stories and reading the Bible with them, he confesses astonishment at the discovery of the indigenous tradition and "the experience of God in oral tradition and with the native religious force that has survived 500 years despite Christianity." This traditional knowledge of God, he writes, "is a millennial experience . . . whose development and profundity fills us today with admiration and respect."[19] I quote Richard's conclusion at some length:

> [T]he Christian Bible has been read and interpreted . . . with a spirit of Hellenistic philosophical abstraction, with the imperialistic spirit of Constantine, with the European spirit of conquest and colonization, with the Western patriarchal and erudite spirit, with the individualistic spirit of modern liberalism. It is necessary to rescue the Bible from this captivity in order to enable another reading and interpretation with the Spirit with which it was written. To do so, we need a *non-occidental* point of reference. . . . My view is that the indigenous peoples, with their culture and religion, are able to give us a non-Western point of

17. Leonardo Boff, *Cry of the Earth, Cry of the Poor* (New York: Orbis, 1997), 114.

18. Boff, *Cry of the Earth*, 123.

19. Pablo Richard, "Indigenous Biblical Hermeneutics: God's Revelation in Native Religions and the Bible (After 500 years of Domination)," in *Text and Experience: Towards a Cultural Exegesis of the Bible*, ed. Daniel Christopher-Smith (Sheffield: Sheffield Academic Press, 1995), 260. It is worth noting that Pablo Richard's commentary on the book of Revelation was the outcome of intensive workshops involving discussions with peasants and indigenous peoples, so that the book of Revelation is read from the perspective of "the poor, indigenous peoples, blacks, women, young people, cosmos and nature, and all those who endure the discrimination of the oppressive and idolatrous system." Pablo Richard, *Apocalypse: A People's Commentary on the Book of Revelation* (Eugene: Wipf and Stock, 1995),3.

> reference. . . . from which we can read and interpret the Bible with newly refreshed eyes, and re-encounter the Spirit in which it was written.[20]

Richard's description of how the interpretation of the Bible has been grossly distorted in the West overlooks the significance of the process of biblical translation into vernacular languages which, according to Lamin Sanneh, created "an overarching series of cultural experiences, *with hitherto obscure cultural systems being thrust into the general stream of universal history.*"[21] Nonetheless, Pablo Richard's discovery of the riches to be found within primal traditions in South America is significant and reflects the fact that tribal peoples throughout the earth, including aboriginal Christians in Australasia and Native American peoples in the United States and Canada, are finding their own voices and demanding to be heard.[22]

There is a further element of the context within which world Christianity has emerged and is now reshaping the church and its mission – the reality of *migration.* This is an era of unprecedented movements of peoples across the world, both *within* nation states and across whole continents, including the massive shifts of population from the southern hemisphere to Europe and North America. Much attention is given to the social, economic, and political outcomes of such mass movements, but the *religious* and *cultural* changes likely to result from what Andrew Walls has called the "great reverse migration" are frequently ignored. However, the presence of large numbers of African, Asian, and Latin American Christians in the cities of Europe and North America means that believers whose faith has been shaped by the interaction between the gospel and primal cultures now present serious challenges to the long-accepted assumption that Western secularisation and materialism

20. Richard, 'Indigenous Biblical Hermeneutics', 271, emphasis original.

21. Sanneh, *Translating the Message,* 2, Emphasis added.

22. On native American traditions, see James Treat, ed., *Native and Christian: Indigenous Voices on Religious Identity in the United States and Canada* (London: Routledge, 1996); and Leanne Betasamosake Simpson, *As We Have Always Done: Indigenous Freedom Through Radical Resistance* (Minneapolis: University of Minnesota Press, 2017). This book is influencing evangelical debates on the future of Christianity in the USA as can be seen in Alan Roxburgh, *Joining God in the Great Unraveling* (Eugene, OR: Cascade, 2021). On the significance of Hispanic perspectives, see Justo Gonzalez, *MANANA: Christian Theology from a Hispanic Perspective* (Nashville: Abingdon, 1990). Virgilio Elizondo's statement in the preface to this important volume accurately describes the present moment in Christian history: "We will no longer impoverish our understanding of God by limiting God to the ways of knowledge of the Western world; we will come to the knowledge of a far greater God by knowing God also through the categories of thought of our own *mestizo* world of Iberoamerica. We can all enrich one another, but no one of us should seek to destroy or compete with the others," 19.

are irreversible. Gerrie ter Haar, concludes that "the rise of African and other non-Western Christian congregations is nothing less than a new phase in the religious history of Europe."[23] In other words, the valuable wisdom of primal religious traditions is not only being rediscovered in places like Northeast India, but at the heart of London, Boston, and even Moscow![24]

Conclusion

Earlier in this chapter I quoted a British missionary to India, William Carey. I want to close by referring to another whose words were spoken a century after Carey, when the character of the missionary movement had changed under the impact of the era of imperial and colonial glory. C. F. (or Charlie) Andrews arrived in India in 1904, but ten years later he resigned his missionary position to move to Rabindranath Tagore's ashram at Santiniketan. Andrews described his own spiritual journey in a sermon preached in the cathedral in Lahore which contained this remarkable passage:

> The question came upon me with a sad, a terrible insistence, as I travelled across many seas, past many shores, whether the modern aggressive, wealthy nations of the world, armed to the teeth against each other, trafficking in the souls of men for gain, can be for long the dwelling place of the meek and lowly Christ; whether the hour may not be near when he says to them. . . . "Woe to you," and will turn instead to the poor, down-trodden peoples of the earth and say unto them, "Come to me." For in his Kingdom, "there are many that are last that shall be first, and first that shall be last."[25]

---

23. Gerrie ter Haar, *Halfway to Paradise: African Christians in Europe* (Cardiff: Cardiff Academic Press, 1998), 3. Elsewhere she has cowritten a significant study of the influence of non-Western religious perspectives on the secular nations of the North as the result of migration. "The growing presence of Africans overseas means that public officials in the European Union and North America will need to develop a serious interest in the religious world-views of the increasing proportion of their populations that is of non-Western origin." Stephen Ellis and Gerrie ter Haar, *Worlds of Power: Religious Thought and Political Practice in Africa* (London: Hurst, 2004), 193.

24. A further example of the discovery of the richness of a primal tradition can be found in Willis Horst, and Ute Paul, and Frank Paul, eds., *Mission without Conquest: An Alternative Missionary Practice* (Carlisle: Langham Literature, 2015). See especially Willis Horst's chapter, "Toba Qom Spirituality: The Remarkable Faith Journey of an Indigenous People in the Argentine Chaco," 25–46.

25. C. F. Andrews quote in Daniel O'Connor, *Gospel, Raj and Swaraj: The Missionary Years of C. F. Andrews, 1904–1914* (Frankfurt: Peter Lang, 1990), 292.

These words now appear to be prophetic of what has transpired during the twentieth century, and we are witnesses to a new phase in both world and Christian history in which peoples from primal traditions will play a crucial role in the emerging mission of world Christianity.

Postscript

When the Saints Come Marching in

Jangkholam Haokip and David W. Smith

The authors of the chapters which make up this book have together attempted to fulfil two broad aims. First, they have addressed the challenges confronting the tribal peoples of Northeast India at a time when that region is experiencing great change. The challenging issues surrounding social, cultural, and religious identity, so characteristic of a postcolonial world, are the subject of passionate and urgent debate. Professor Xaxa's comprehensive survey of the recent history and development of this region sets the scene for the subsequent studies and provides an invaluable overview of the context which is likely to be especially helpful for readers who are previously unfamiliar with the area and its peoples.

The studies which follow, particularly in the second half of the book, focus attention on the cultural and religious traditions of the tribal peoples, exploring their ancient myths and folklore and the relationship between these beliefs and values and the Christianity which has been widely accepted since the arrival of Western missionaries during the colonial era. While some of our authors focus attention on the urgent task of preserving core aspects of the ancient traditions, including both myths and music, others wrestle with the same issues from the perspective of the new faith, asking how it can be contextualised, or to use the Catholic term, enculturated within tribal society. It is evident that for our contributors, these issues are not academic or theoretical. The urgency of the task of constructing an identity in which religious conversion is perceived to fulfil rather than to destroy peoples' ancient cultural heritages is created by the need for both connection to the story of the past and by the growing conviction that the wisdom embedded within these traditions has something of crucial importance to offer the modern world.

One theme which recurs throughout these studies concerns the contrast between oral and literate cultures. Songram Basumatary describes the crucial importance of oral tradition for his Boro people and demonstrates how oral performance acts as a "sacred text," linking the present with the past and relating a living tradition to the existential challenges now arising in a rapidly changing and globalised world.

An aspect of this topic which has not been mentioned so far and really should be introduced here concerns recent shifts in the scholarship of the New Testament with the emergence of what has been called "biblical performance criticism." This approach cannot be described in detail here, but it involves the growing recognition that the world of Jesus and his followers, of Paul and John of Patmos, was one in which *oral tradition was everywhere pervasive and dominant.* It has been estimated that in the first-century world of the Roman Empire, only three percent of the Jewish population in Palestine was literate and that the "texts" which shaped most people's lives "were coins and occasional words on graves or buildings." By contrast, the spoken word reached everyone. Given this cultural context, a growing number of scholars question long-held assumptions concerning the authorship of much of the New Testament, arguing that there is evidence that the story of Jesus, as told in Mark's Gospel, for instance, was composed "not by individual authors with pens in hand, but orally in performance; that is they were shaped in the telling."[1]

The implications of this shift within biblical scholarship concerning the origins of the Gospels are massive, and they have particular importance in relation to the central concerns of this present book. Orality, long dismissed in the Western world as a kind of survival from an age now left behind by the process of evolution and devalued by being classified as *illiteracy,* now reappears as crucial to the foundation of the gospel traditions and as a form of communication capable of expressing truth in ways that writing cannot do. The importance of oral tradition within Northeast India is repeatedly asserted by our authors, and it is likely that they would be in agreement with the words of the Catholic scholar Anthony Gittens who says,

> [F]ew people in highly literate cultures understand that literacy itself is limited, that its opposite is not *illiteracy* but *orality*, and

1. These are the words of Antionette Clark Wire in her ground-breaking book, *The Case for Mark Composed in Performance* (Eugene, OR: Cascade, 2001), 2.

> that in a predominantly oral world, many aspects of literacy are redundant. Jesus lived among people who were predominantly and functionally oral, and his message did not require them to read but to listen *and to be engaged.*[2]

This quote brings us to the second broad aim of the authors of this book: while their primary concern is with the local context of Northeast India, they also intend that a wider, international readership be made aware of the situation of tribal Christians in this region, and are thus given the opportunity to recognise the spiritual riches which those believers have to offer to a still emerging world Christianity. Elsewhere in Asia new theological voices have been raised insisting that "the collapse of Euro-American (Western) dominance of theology" provides the opportunity for "an increased recognition of a polycentric world and a polycentric world Christianity, with emphasis on many theological centres." They add that the future beckons "for a truly catholic Christianity that honors unity-in-diversity in both church and theology."[3]

It is the humble conviction of the writers of the preceding chapters that Christians in Northeast India have their part to play in the world Christian movement, and that along with the millions of disciples of Christ from primal cultures across Asia, Africa, and both South and North America, they may offer their testimony among those who worship Christ from "every tribe and language and people and nation" (Rev 5:9).

2. Anthony Gittens, Catholic Theological Union, Chicago in commendation of Wire's book *Case for Mark*, 226, emphasis original. See also James A. Maxey, *From Orality to Orality: A New Paradigm for Contextual Translation of the Bible* (Eugene, OR: Cascade, 2009).

3. T. D. Gener and L. Bautista, "Theological Method," in *Global Dictionary of Theology*, eds. William Dyrness and Veli-Matti Karkkainen (Downers Grove, IL: IVP Academic, 2008), 890.

Langham Literature and its imprints are a ministry of Langham Partnership.

Langham Partnership is a global fellowship working in pursuit of the vision God entrusted to its founder John Stott –

> ***to facilitate the growth of the church in maturity and Christ-likeness through raising the standards of biblical preaching and teaching.***

Our vision is to see churches in the Majority World equipped for mission and growing to maturity in Christ through the ministry of pastors and leaders who believe, teach and live by the word of God.

Our mission is to strengthen the ministry of the word of God through:

- nurturing national movements for biblical preaching
- fostering the creation and distribution of evangelical literature
- enhancing evangelical theological education

especially in countries where churches are under-resourced.

Our ministry

Langham Preaching partners with national leaders to nurture indigenous biblical preaching movements for pastors and lay preachers all around the world. With the support of a team of trainers from many countries, a multi-level programme of seminars provides practical training, and is followed by a programme for training local facilitators. Local preachers' groups and national and regional networks ensure continuity and ongoing development, seeking to build vigorous movements committed to Bible exposition.

Langham Literature provides Majority World preachers, scholars and seminary libraries with evangelical books and electronic resources through publishing and distribution, grants and discounts. The programme also fosters the creation of indigenous evangelical books in many languages, through writer's grants, strengthening local evangelical publishing houses, and investment in major regional literature projects, such as one volume Bible commentaries like *The Africa Bible Commentary* and *The South Asia Bible Commentary*.

Langham Scholars provides financial support for evangelical doctoral students from the Majority World so that, when they return home, they may train pastors and other Christian leaders with sound, biblical and theological teaching. This programme equips those who equip others. Langham Scholars also works in partnership with Majority World seminaries in strengthening evangelical theological education. A growing number of Langham Scholars study in high quality doctoral programmes in the Majority World itself. As well as teaching the next generation of pastors, graduated Langham Scholars exercise significant influence through their writing and leadership.

To learn more about Langham Partnership and the work we do visit **langham.org**

www.ingramcontent.com/pod-product-compliance
Lightning Source LLC
Chambersburg PA
CBHW070539170426
43200CB00011B/2483

* 9 7 8 1 8 3 9 7 3 5 3 4 9 *